Lucy on Lea

Lucy on Leave…….

by

Lucy Verinder

ISBN: 978-0-9935575-5-2

Lucy on Leave.......

by

Lucy Verinder

ISBN: 978-0-9935575-5-2

Copyright Lucy Verinder 2016

All rights reserved. No part of this publication maybe reproduced, stored in a retrieval system or transmitted in any form or by any means, electronic, mechanical, photo-copy, recording or otherwise, without prior written consent of the copyright owner. Nor can it be circulated in any form of binding or cover other than that in which it is published and without similar condition including this condition being imposed on a subsequent purchaser.

The right of Lucy Verinder to be identified as the author of this work has been asserted in accordance with the Copyright Designs and Patents Act 1988

A copy of this book is deposited with the British Library

Published by

i2i Publishing. Manchester. UK.

www.i2ipublishing.co.uk

Cover illustration by Bazmac:

http://bazmac26.wix.com/pictor-illustration

Chapter 1.

Cancer is a C**t

These are two words beginning with 'C' for you for starters.

Here are a few more;
Calcification,
Carcinoma,
Carcinogenic,
(Coffee is apparently – well fuck that – I like coffee – so join the party in my right boob as apparently it is all kicking off in there.)

I say 'apparently' because until yesterday I was 'fine'. One doctor's appointment, one mammogram, one scan, one biopsy and now I am not fine. From swaggering into hospital feeling superciliously sorry for everyone else to having a nurse stroke my arm during the biopsy – *don't fucking stroke my arm,* I thought – *I am fine, it doesn't hurt, you bitch* – even though I was pretending it did but I was fine with it, to look hard – I am now feeling a bit sorry for myself as I have breast cancer. BREAST CANCER!!!!!!! HELP!!! RUN AWAY!!! CRY!!! LAUGH???? Certainly laugh when the surgeon said 'it' is 13cm like he was going to give me first prize at a show for the best home-grown tumour over 6 months – plus he had probably the pinkest tongue I have ever witnessed in my entire life that he kept rolling out of his mouth which meant I wasn't really listening to what he was saying. Anyway, day one is, 'concerning presentation from the scan'; biopsy results back on Thursday when the surgeons meet to discuss my treatment. I picture them sitting round a big wooden table in some dark wood-panelled hospital room with my name on the agenda, "And so we come to Lucy Verinder, how fucked do we think she is my friends?"

Fairly fucked I know already, as I have to have a mastectomy, they have pretty much told me that. A nice sounding word; soft and motherly, somewhat disguising the truth which is you are going to have your tit lopped off and it is going to be fucking painful!!! Which is a shame really as I like my right boob, but I suppose given the fact that I have had a baby and breast-fed and had loads of sex it has had a good innings. If I was to write a list of essential body parts required for remainder of life I suppose it would come fairly low down. That is positive thinking my friends.

Cliché; there is another c word with which to end day one as I am keeping a journal and I haven't done that since I was 16 and my Mum read it and discovered I was in love with my art teacher. No more journals for me for 20 plus years; cancer and coffee.

Chapter 2.

Pleasure and Pain

Today was going to be S words – STEAMING PILE OF SHIT for example, until I realised that psychosomatic started with a p so let's do P today; pleasure and pain. Pleasure as I am not at work and I don't like work and today is a stunningly beautiful day which means that instead of squinting myopically at a tiny DHL computer screen and worrying about internally invented deadlines (Tues will do for now) that I don't actually give a shit about, I am walking round a lake picking sloes to make sloe gin which my darkly humorous husband (thank the lord) says I may not be around to drink – thanks for that. I even bought an ice-cream, (tra-la-la-la-la) amusingly the ice-cream man appeared to be asleep in his van and misheard me and gave me a Magnum apple strudel, which apparently is an ice-cream but shouldn't be. The sloes were, as in all pleasurable pursuits, not plentiful enough to be taken for granted. Some old bat stopped me while I was picking them to ask why they weren't yellow! Yellow? Who has ever seen any berries that are yellow that are giving out fucking vibes to pick them, you stupid cow. She was gripping onto my carrier bag while I was trying to explain how you make sloe gin and I thought at one point she expected me to give her my pickings so I lied and said that you need to make them with two bags of sugar to half a bottle of gin which if she believed me should make for some pretty shit sloe gin.

Spoke to my sister today as well – it feels like you are off-loading information, which is a help, and not a help. This is because loved ones want good news and there isn't any. She advised me to speak to one of the hospital breast care nurses to make sure I had my facts straight; so I did and I had. She just told me the same things in a slightly more 'nursey,' softer way but basically I am still fucked.

Other pleasures today; playing pool with Tom whom I beat; I also beat a lovely (and I suspect lonely) chap who took the winner on. Interestingly, and cliché number 2; normally I would get all embarrassed and fall apart playing pool against a stranger, but guess what; the joy of cancer is that that reaction seems mightily pathetic given the hardness required here. So to the pain, which I believe is all psychosomatic as today, I am in no doubt that I also have liver cancer, slightly yellow skin in the bathroom mirror, bone cancer, back hurts and lung cancer, out of breath going upstairs!!! Six months I give myself!!!!!!!

Proper pain is only the small hole in my breast which I found myself caring about, which is a bit stupid considering it won't be there at all in a few weeks; pleasure and pain.

Chapter 3.

Walking and Worrying

Its words beginning with 'W' today; walked around Newmillerdam in the sunshine, lovely; worrying that I am going to lose my lunch because I learn something today.

If you walk round a parkland lake with a very large Melton Mowbray Pie in your hand, everyone that walks past you will immediately realise what they really, really want is a very large Melton Mowbray Pie. At one point it was virtually snatched out my hand by a famished five-year old. Cathedral Cheddar cheese got there first with that one, I suppose.

Told Emily today; she had already sensed the truth; more tears, then common sense, then humour.

Emily; "Well, when I told my friend you might have cancer she said, well, my Dad DOES have cancer AND he has to have tests EVERY week, now I can tell her you do too." Bloody hell, cancer is apparently cool and gives your bragging rights!!!

Then in New Look amongst all the teenage 'lippy' t-shirts sarcastically saying things like, 'I'm out of bed, what more do you want?' Emily says; "Do you think they have t-shirts saying, 'I've got cancer so what are you gonna do about it?'" And finally, "Mum, can we not call it cancer? Let's call it Carrots?" So from today I have been diagnosed with Carrots. The future is bright; the future is orange.

Chapter 4.

Ironing and Irony

'I' is today's letter. 'I' is for ironing and irony. I like ironing. It appeals to my sense of perfection; sad but true. I am ironing while watching the most cringe-worthy programme I have ever seen. It is called 'Real Housewives of Atlanta.' At first I thought it was actors then I realised women do really live these lives. Great TV but a tragic indictment of human nature, or at least American human nature! One woman had just moved to LA, into her dream apartment amongst the stars and was in hysterics because she could only fit six out of her eight prized (and utterly hideous) statues round the fucking pool! I think she was called Sasha – her strap line was, "I gotta lotta Sas; I gotta a lotta Ass, you'll do as I ask!" Er, no.

Irony; the fact that my private health care package, if I don't go for private care, is going to pay me up to £5k a year to use the NHS. It seems I have a get ill, get rich quick, scheme available to me.

The final observation of the day is how revealing and funny peoples' reactions are to the news. Poor Tom spent most of the day fielding off misplaced but well-meant sympathy. The best one from a lady who asked whether he would like some food parcels!! WTF!! As he politely pointed out if there is going to be one area of struggle for Tom over the next few months it's not going to be on the food front given the fact that I haven't cooked him a meal in 25 fucking years!!! Food parcels?? Superb.

Chapter 5.

Pets and Puddings

Went for a lovely walk today. I made the mistake of playing that 'betting game' everyone finds themselves doing every now and again; usually against something frivolous; for example – if I get to the end of the road before another blue car goes past I will get this promotion. Today's was for higher stakes; if I can get round the park and get everyone I pass to look up and smile and say hello to me then Tuesday will be on the better end of bad news. Odds should be pretty high given that my park is situated in the heart of West Yorkshire not the Home Counties. Needless to say; 10 dog walkers to the good and with home in sight I passed a sour faced lady who didn't even look up as I approached – OH NO! SO CLOSE! but then, glory be, her lovely little Yorkshire Terrier scuttled up to me, jumped up to my knee and gave me the best Northern smile you could wish for – this would never happen down south for a number of reasons – so bring on Tuesday I am good to go!

Emily wants a pet. I don't want a pet. I don't want Emily to be sad. Emily knows this and has leverage. I appear to have promised her a gerbil. I really don't like gerbils. I really don't like gerbils for a number of reasons which I won't go into expect to say that the last one we had was posthumously named Fang and made his great escape by pushing aside two volumes of books. How? By holding the lid of his cage down and then scoffing a whole chilli plant on his way to freedom. Safe to say a pet is still in negotiation. As I write we have managed to bring Emily round to our views on gerbils and we are now discussing the merits of a tortoise.

Me: no fangs, no fur and not fast.

Emily: a pet. To be continued…

Went out for a lovely meal with Tom. Too much white wine (or was it too little) too much romance (never too little) and lots of laughter, especially when my millionaire shortbread desert arrived (prepare yourself for some dark humour) looking exactly like a fucking breast on a plate – bad enough until the waitress poured hot toffee sauce over it and it literally shrunk in size while bubbling strangely. Safe to say I don't need to spell out what we were thinking. The restaurant was small and quiet and our laughter was loud and dark – don't mind us everyone, we are just in fits over how much my wife's desert looks like her calcified tit will look during chemo. I suppose millionaire short bread sounds a tad more appetising than chocolate breast with chemo sauce!

Chapter 6.

Crouching Tiger, Hidden Terrier

D-Day today. D for diagnosis. A day of acronyms and analogies. Firstly, to the acronyms. DCIS, IDC, HER2, H6R2 negative etc., etc., etc. I am not a fan of acronyms as my working life has been blighted by them. There are four specific types; the first are the acronyms to disguise very boring work practices (ATDVBWP). For a start I work for a company called DHL. Everyone thinks the D stands for Deutsche Post, but the H and L? Not a bloody clue. Hitler? Laundry? And guess what? You will be amazed to know it actually stands for 'Dalsey, Hullblom, Lynn' who were the founding members. Interesting? Not really.

Within the world of DHL there lurks a whole wonderful world of acronyms for boring and complicated practice.

I will give you an example. I heard the following statement a number of weeks ago from a colleague; "You will need to load your BCA onto LADB in time for the GPRB review if you want to avoid a CAPA and a CCP. What the Fuck? Or rather WTF!!!???"

Then there are the acronyms to create words that make things sound cooler (ATCWTMTSC). RADA is one of these. Everyone knows it stands for the Royal Academy of Dramatic Arts. The problem is this doesn't sound very dramatic or arty. RADA on the other hand makes way for the dramatic flick of the hair, the wave of the artistic hand and the comment, "I went to RADA, darling you know." Perfect.

The third type is the bloody obvious and needless acronym (TBOANA). You see this all the time in the press. For example; "Today, Bill Beaumont, the Chairman of the Rugby Football Union - in brackets, the RFU said England would whip the Aussies on Saturday." Well, thank you so much for that vital piece of additional information, without which you would have totally lost me! And finally to the best kind of acronyms, the acronyms that accidentally spell out rude words (ATASORW). The number one spot for me goes to the Central University of Newcastle Upon Tyne!

And so to my acronyms; hiding the news, which was no worse and no better than expected. It was delivered to me and my husband by a fantastic gentleman surgeon called Dr Sowdi, with both medical straightness, compassion and a large dose of Chinese spiritual wisdom. But we weren't fooled because this man was clearly Yoda. I say this for a number of reasons. Firstly, minus the ears (obviously) he looked remarkably like him. Secondly, he was clearly between 300 and 400 galactic years of age and thirdly he channelled his advice and prognosis to us in the following way; (Adopt Yoda-esque voice)

"Your cancer is as a tiger. He is in the garden. He is angry and fierce but I am going to shoot him dead (ok?) You may think having an angry tiger in your garden is worse than having a tenacious terrier in your garden? He paused – we nodded dutifully. Yes, because this terrier can hide. I may not be able to shoot him and so when he gets to your kitchen he will cause havoc.

So there we are. A new Chinese Proverb;

> *The man who kills tiger in garden live long life; the man who lets terrier in kitchen, not so long.*

Chapter 7.

Hair, Suits and Rolling Pins

1. Hair

One of the surprises I have had over the last few days as I 'research' this illness is how high on the list of trauma the subject of hair loss is. Ssssshhh! Yes, hair loss. Whisper it. You lose your hair when you have chemo. EVERYBODY KNOWS THIS FACT. What I find strange is that given the list of painful and scary treatments and associated side effects of cancer treatment, hair loss comes so high. I have done my research on this one so trust me; losing your hair does not hurt!

Now, I am not belittling people's affection for their hair but for me I am okay with it. This is because my hair (for reference, I am referring to hair in all its bodily glory, not just head hair) is having a bloody laugh with me in recent years. Those of you who are 40+ will know what I am referring to. Before this age, hair, for the majority of people, pretty much behaves itself; i.e. it grows where it is socially acceptable to grow and not where it is not. However, as you cross your fortieth bridge (or there about) your hair starts to take the piss big time. Hair starts to grow in all the wrong places - chin, upper lip etc. (obviously only a problem for the female species) and for men; ears, nose and monobrows (not a good look even for left wing politicians.) The cruel irony (predominantly if you are a man) is that while hair is suddenly fascinated in growing in strange places it starts to lose interest in growing where you want it to – i.e. your head. As the years go by, the time I spend plucking, waxing, shaving etc. to stem the hairy tide is becoming unacceptable. Don't get me wrong I am not the fucking bearded lady but with the exception of our French Friends, having hairy armpits is just simply not de rigueur.

The second laugh my hair has had with me is that it can't now be bothered to maintain its colour. I am not greying I am whiting. This leaves me facing three possible follicle paths. The first, I like to call the 'The Germaine Greer'. This look is designed to put two feminist fingers up to the male dominated, shallow and youth-centric world and says quite simply, "I don't give a fuck about the fact I am old and grey for I am too busy being cerebral." Now, on a sliding beauty scale from Angelina Jolie to Hilary Mantel (sorry, Hilary) I put myself at the top end of the bottom half. Basically, I am not ready for my 'Germaine' era quite yet.

The second follicle path available to me I call 'The Christine Lagarde.' Unlike 'The Greer,' this look also tells the word that you don't give a fuck you are greying but due to your monumental natural chic-ness you still look completely fabulous (because, of course you very much do give a fuck and have spent thousands on getting the I don't give a fuck look). Men, I know, it's complicated. The 'Lagarde' can be pulled off with increased aplomb if you are a) powerful b) French and c) can afford an expensive all year round tan. I am none of these so 'The Lagarde' is closed to me.

So, like well over 90% of the female population my only remaining realistic choice is to dye (no pun intended). As a result, sadly my hair now has three resplendent colour variations which I am aware is fooling nobody; namely, the remains of my natural colour (basically brown), my dyed hair (an attempt to match) and the endlessly resilient white hair that usually, 3 of 4 weeks after spending 10 times more money than is sensible, bravely pushes on through, as white as the day is long. So, in summary bring on hair loss; the hairy tide of unwanted follicles will be stemmed and my plucky head of white will be no more. And you never know it might grow back as a perfect and effortless 'Lagarde'!!! Hoorah!!!

2. Suits and Rolling Pins

I like my local, council gym. I used to like to go after work. I now like to go in during the day. Going during the day, has however, revealed a new face to my gym. For the majority of the overworked and stressed population the gym is visited in the evening. During this time the gym is predominantly full of healthy, shiny, happy people; nothing wrong with that. However, in the day it is a vastly different and frankly disturbing experience. In the day my gym is full of the fat, the unfortunate and the frankly bizarre. Don't get me wrong, being fat can be due to other causes beyond being lazy and eating too much so I am not mocking I am just observing.

Today I saw the following; a gentleman on the rowing machine in a three-piece suit. It was a serious suit and he was rowing seriously. Now, unless I have missed a very strange development in Adidas breathe easy sportswear, there is simply no explanation here. This, however, is nothing compared to the gentleman working out with a rolling pin in the weights room. Again, it is Gods honest truth. He was using the rolling pin to massage his muscles head to toe in a method that he had clearly refined over many sessions. The question that begs is why come to the fucking gym to do this given that the last time I looked standard gym equipment did not extend to kitchenware. And finally to perhaps the most intriguing workout vision of the day. Sitting under the men's push up machine was a lady that I can only kindly describe as latitudinally challenged. It appeared that she had set up camp under the machine some time ago as she had conveniently used one end of the 100kg dumb bell to hang her rucksack and the other end her hand bag. She seemed very content and not remotely tempted to do any exercise (God forbid). The final piece de resistance, however, was the fact, that as I was leaving the gym I looked back to see if she was still there and saw her reach into her rucksack and pull out a cheese sandwich and a can of coke! Work it girl.

Chapter 8.

Hair Today, Gone Tomorrow: Further Follicle Musings

Over my life I realise that hair, both mine and other peoples, has played a part in some bad memories. Here are a few.

1. **Giving Birth**

At the point I was giving birth to my daughter, and I mean literally at the point of giving birth to my daughter, specifically I mean the moment when all women without fail think, "This is simply not fucking physically possible!" I heard my midwife turn to her colleague and whisper, "Blimey! We could pull this one out by its hair!" Now, I remember I was drugged up on gas and air. I have to inform you that for the past 6 hours I had been convinced I was so thirsty because I was actually giving birth in the Australian Outback. I was mortified and heard to wail, "I am not going to give birth to a fucking marsupial!"

(Postscript: She was actually a beautiful baby girl but she did have a head of black hair thicker than my husband's.)

2. **Classroom Bully**

In the 80's hair was complicated. Big hair winged up with hairspray; good. Pencilled in eyebrows; good. Lady side burns; bad. I had side burns. Sitting in class while my nemesis got all my lovely class mates to hang felt tip pens from the sides of their faces was cruel and not particularly funny. The main insult being the pathetic inaccuracy given that my sideburns were neither blue, plastic nor the length of a bloody Berol pen. Despite this, I got the message and promptly shaved them off when I got home. Happy days.

3. Nudist Beach

We used to go to France and Germany on holiday as a family. I don't specifically remember a formal conversation about whether we all wanted to go to a nudist beach but never the less we found ourselves on a German beach for the sartorially abstaining. Now, the thing about nudist beaches is that in your mind's eye you see ample breasted lovelies and tight pecked hunks etc. etc. The reality is tragically and disappointingly nothing like. The beach was literally crawling with hideous and frighteningly hairy overweight Germans indulging in a spot of Freikorperkultur. As I looked up from where I was sunbathing the sun was completely blocked out by a pair of the most monumentally hairy bollocks swinging proudly past as fucking Adolf Koch (Google it) strutted on by. These things can scar you for life.

Chapter 9.

Malapropisms, Misunderstandings and Mrs Leg

1.Malapropisms

I phoned my hairdressers this morning to make an appointment and the lady who answered the phone said, "Hello, cancer help you?" Er, pardon me? Well, that is definitely what I thought I heard. Either way it has got me thinking about the wonderful world of malapropisms. I love malapropisms. We can thank Richard Brinsley Sheridan for his Mrs Malaprop character (don't bother looking up the comedy, it is dreadful). Nowadays malapropisms tend to originate from either ignorance or idiocy, or both. This is why on the whole children between the ages of three and seven are such masters of the art. I have been collecting my daughter's finest moments for years (she is now 11 and she won't thank me for it). Below are the best:

On Food and Drink:

"Mummy can I have some straggled eggs on toast?

On Life and Religion:

"Do you know when you die you go to Devon?"
"What does Honolulu praise the Lord mean?"
"Is Hull the opposite of Heaven?"

On Health and Beauty:

"I don't want to grow my hair long, Mummy, 'cos if you keep it short you don't get woodlice"
"Isn't Grandma having a laxative time?"

"Did you know if someone stays in bed all day they are called a noc-terminal"

On History and Nature:

"Do chimpanzees have disposable thumbs too?"

"Did you know in Victorian times a 7-year-old girl actually died of the Weasels"?

And finally, probably the best of the lot from Emily's cousin upon returning from a day at school:

"Mum, it's alright if you choke on an apple from now on because today I learnt the Hind Leg Removal."

While children obviously have an excuse for coming out with malapropisms there are not really any excuses for Presidents of the United States of America. 'Bushisms' are now as much part of our lexicon as malapropisms which, when you think about it, is very scary given my child was pre-school age and pretty powerless and Mr George W Bush was arguably the most powerful man in the Western World. His many utterances are well documented but my absolute favourite story was, apparently, at the first White House correspondents' dinner in 2001, Bush proudly read out from the first book of 'Bushisms' and boasted that he was responsible for inventing the term 'misunderstanded'. THE TOTAL BUFFOON! He had meant to say he had invented the term 'mis-underestimated'. He had actually managed to malaprop his own malapropism!!! What a total tit.

2.Misunderstandings

These memories are more misunderstandings rather than true malapropisms but no less funny for it.

During my first meal out with my less than un-intimidating future Mother and Father in Law, I was struggling to decide what to order as a starter. "Why don't you have the Beef Tomatoes with a Salad?" offered my (then) boyfriend helpfully. "But I am a vegetarian!" I replied (yes, I know). Silence.

My food faux pas is, however, beaten hands down by the lady at the next table during another meal, whom I overheard enquiring politely to the waiter as to whether he could tell her what was in her 'tuna knicker say' (Tuna Nicoise to you and I).

One day at work my very clever and hardworking French Graduate Placement asked if she could have five minutes with me for a chat. She looked worried. She said she had a problem with me. Now, I use a lot of unnecessary business metaphors; it's wrong but I can't help it. I am not proud of it but I have definitely done 'blue sky thinking' in my time and am certainly guilty of collective 'brain storming' (I did once hear this called cerebral showering - WTF!!) Anyway, my lovely colleague's big problem was, despite her commendable grasp of the English Language she simply did not understand my metaphoric madness. More to the point she did not realise that they were not to be taken literally. The poor girl was exhausted. She had been trying to 'row her own boat', while 'shooting for the stars' and 'thinking out of the box', for bloody months.

She was at breaking point. God knows what she had thought last week when I told her to stop 'beating around the bush.'

3.Mrs Leg

And so to Mrs Leg. Dear, old, selfless Mrs Leg. When my sisters and I were growing up and we had all stuffed our faces with firsts of one of Mum's delicious trifles, which meant there was not enough left over for everyone to have seconds, my Mum was oft to be heard uttering the selfless and kind words, "Don't worry dear family, I will be 'Mrs Leg'". She would go without seconds. We would all nod sagely, because we knew. To be 'Mrs Leg' was internationally understood to mean you were altruistic and kind and selfless, putting others hunger and needs before your own. It was clever, you see, because it came from the 'olden times' when a large family would be enjoying a roast chicken but unfortunately there wasn't enough of the breast meat to go round so the caring mother would put her children first and be the martyr; be the "Mrs Leg" and literally offer to have the leg meat rather than the better quality white meat. I liked this version but I preferred my own embellishment. I imagined Mrs Leg as an old lady, dressed in an ill-fitting woollen coat, maybe even a bobble hat. You know the kind of slightly batty neighbour we all have, who invites herself round to number 2 and then had to be asked to stay for tea and she would say; "No, no, I won't, just a cup of tea will do, I don't want to be any trouble." Even though she was lonely and probably a bit hungry, she was Mrs Leg you see. In fact, when I really went to town on this, I sometimes imagined the globally famous Mrs Leg finally relinquishing and staying for tea – roast chicken – of course. Not enough to go round- of course, and offering to have the leg. Mrs Leg being Mrs Leg! Brilliant!

But there is a problem here isn't there Mum and Dad? Yes. BECAUSE "I'LL BE MRS LEG" IS NOT A FUCKING INTERNATIONALLY KNOWN AND LOVED SAYING IS IT??? NO. Outside the wonderful Wareham family world nobody has ever heard of Mrs Fucking Leg, never mind offered to be the modern embodiment of her, have they?

So, about the time that my sisters and I learnt the sad news about Father Christmas, did Mum put a caring and maternal arm around our shoulders and break the news about Mrs Leg? No she did not. Instead she sent us out into the cruel and unforgiving wide world, innocent of this critical fact, and awaiting our inevitable public shaming.

It was only a matter of time. Picture the scene. My husband and I are having dinner with our sophisticated and worldly friends. It is roast chicken (oh, no) - there is not enough breast to go round (yes, it's coming)................me, "Don't worry, my friends", I announce proudly, "for I will be Mrs Leg!"

SILENCE.

MORE SILENCE...

STILL MORE SILENCE.......................................

Excuse me, says my husband, “but who the fuck is Mrs Leg!!??” It took some explaining.

Chapter 10.

Puberty, pro bono and Pre-ops

1. Puberty

My daughter is going through puberty. Surprisingly there are similarities between what she is going through and what I am going through. Two worlds collide; the old one is very lovely and simple. The new one; not so much.

Despite what Disney World, Florida would have us believe, puberty is not quite as simple as hanging on to a much loved pair of Nemo socks. It is more complicated than that. In Emily's childhood world Mum and Dad are easy to love; all seeing all giving, God like figures. It is a gorgeous world of Lego and Fruit Shoots; SpongeBob and bath time, bear hugs and tickles, fish fingers and swing parks. The new world is very different. It is more complex and confusing. A world of YouTube and bras; pimples and dry shampoo, hockey practice and homework, bitching and boyfriends. Worse, these two worlds do not take turns nicely. They mix it up big time. And not even day to day; I am talking minute to minute. As I write Emily is playing with her Lego while watching her iPad, sitting in her bra and knickers looking about 14, and she has just told me she loves me and hates me in the same bloody sentence. Apparently puberty can take up to three years to pass. Lovely.

2. Pro Bono

Over the last few weeks, in addition to my favourite pastimes of writing this and being with my daughter I am watching a lot more TV. In my past life I didn't have time to watch classy American drama box sets. I do now. There are consequences however; I now have a prime time TV sized crush on Harvey Specter. If you have watched 'Suits' you will know exactly who I am talking about. If you haven't, well, then you won't. 'Suits' provides a 25-minute indulgent escapism into the utterly ridiculous, silky, smooth edged world of Pearson Hardman, a New York Legal firm. To be employed here you need to be three things; off the scale physically beautiful, have an endless oeuvre of sharp witted put downs, and be monumentally bright. When I say bright I don't mean just Harvard genius. These people can be handed a 44-page case file and they need to do no more than nonchalantly glance down at the first page for 2 or 3 seconds and they have magically absorbed the whole bloody thing and are now ready to talk victory tactics and pocket their fee. These people are grey matter wizards, it's just brilliant. Spinning splendidly in the centre of this world is the wonderful Harvey. Aaaah, swoon, Harvey; resplendent in his thirteen grand double breasted suits, with his lasciviously sweet upper lip and justifiable self-confidence; Harvey is who everybody wants to be (male) or be with (female). As Harvey would say, "It's not bragging if it's true." I could quite happily spend the rest of my days curled quietly up on his sofa in his gorgeous penthouse-esque office while he works long into another night. Or, putting it another way I would serpina his pro bono any day of the week. Sorry.

3. Pre-Op

Pre-op appointment today. My hospital is a PFI which means it is new and shiny and looks; smells and feels like an airport. In no small part due to the fact that when you go in you enter a huge well-lit atrium and wait for your name and gate number to flash up on the big screen. *Lucy Verinder please proceed to gate* 22. Unfortunately, rather than grabbing a cheeky beer and snacks for the flight, this time I take my appointment letter and make my way to the breast cancer clinic. Not quite so much fun.

Chapter 11.

Destination: Hospital over night

My operation is booked for the 22nd of October, first thing in the morning; in the diary and not movable. The care and support for me from the nurses has been incredible. I am as ready as anyone can ever be for having surgery. I have been into hospital overnight three times in my life to date. These have all been quite unique experiences.

The first time was when my early on-set glaucoma was worryingly misdiagnosed as a brain tumour. I spent a night on a lovely ward in what I can only describe as a white breeze block cubicle with easy roll in roll off access for my bed (it was clear why). The dark hours were spent listening to the horrific wails of the lady in the 'cubicle' next door who they were trying to save the life of as her liver failed. They failed. I was usefully informed afterwards, she was a long term alcohol and she had been a regular; lovely. I was eventually seen by the duty doctor at about 2am who, given the fact he appeared to be acutely unwell, (he had to keep leaving my bedside to cough into a bucket), may only have had slightly better odds of surviving to the morning than the patients on his ward; happy days.

The second time I stayed overnight in hospital was after giving birth to my daughter. The three nights I was staying in hospital were for no more serious symptoms than knackered-ness. Not due to the fact I had just given birth but because I had the ironic joy (given the fact that my beloved husband is partial to the odd snoring session) of being in the bed next to a lady who had an off the scale vibrating soft pallet. I am talking, pneumatic drill with a bit of close up blender here. The ward sister eventually took pity on me and moved Emily and I to a private room. Lovely for us, not so lovely for Tom when he came to visit in the morning and no-one had told him why neither of us were in our beds.

My next two post-birth nights in recovery were spent getting a rude awaking from my middle class, ignorant point of view that all babies born in hospital are wanted, adored and have been created by couples who also want and adore each other; equally that they appreciate and respect the fact that they have just safely given birth in a hospital, for free and that the process hasn't resulted in them, and/or, their baby dying. This is not the case. The couple in the next bed were having a heated row over paternity which ended with the beautiful line; "Well, it can't be fucking mine, its fucking ginger!" The next equally high-brow conversation I overheard was a woman on her phone at the top of her voice demanding her family to get her checked out immediately on medical grounds. I believe her words were; "Get me fucking out of here! Now! All the Doctors are fucking Paki's. I'm not gonna be fucking felt up by a fucking Paki!" You could not make it up.

My most recent visit was when Emily had a mild asthma attack and needed to be kept in overnight for observation. Emily has virally induced asthma. This means she has asthma but she doesn't, and that she needs a nebulizer but can't have one – until she has an attack that is. Not ideal. Emily was fine and slept like a baby. I was not. It became clear about 1 am that as the mother of the patient whether I got any sleep or not was of no medical concern whatsoever. Now, I accept, there are those that would agree; given that my daughter was being monitored through the night for oxygen levels in the blood to the brain, a good night's sleep should not be at the top of my priorities. And I agree, but I didn't even have a bloody chair! Around 2.30am I sleepily eyed a fold-up bed at the end of the ward that looked like a cross between a small combined harvester and a Victorian torture device. I politely asked the, not so pleasant ward sister whether I could put it down. Her words were," If you must". However, her expression said, "You, weak, pathetic mother, what do think this place is, fucking Premier Inn? Do you think Lenny Henry is going to waltz in any minute to fluff up your fucking pillows?" I smiled politely and sat back meekly on the side of the bed. Matron had spoken.

Chapter 12.

Non-stick Electrodes and Prosthetic Breasts

Things you don't expect to be doing before lunch on a Monday morning; perusing the shelves of my lovely nurse's extensive prosthetic breast collection for starters. I haven't had so much fun in a long time. My only slight criticism of her is the fact that I believe if your aim is to put to rest the mind of your average – to – small-chested patient who is about to require one of these creations, you need to break her in gently. Don't, for example, proudly whip out a 42 fucking TRIPLE F prosthetic beauty as sample number one, and then hand it to your patient to 'have a feel'. I had quite simply never seen (or felt) anything like it in my life (real or otherwise). I was quite overwhelmed. Honest to God this thing was bigger than Blencathra. It was magnificent. I nearly keeled over when she handed it me. It was heavier than a baby. Jesus Christ, how do big breasted women even get out of the bed in the morning? I did finally manage to wrestle it back down onto my nurse's desk and sit down exhausted. Strangely, I got an overwhelming urge to pat it. To show it who was boss. So when my nurse wasn't looking, I did. It wobbled gloriously. I wanted to take it home with me. I am hoping my modest 34B 'prosthy' pet might be a bit easier to tame.

Next to bloods and ECG scan, Bloods; easy. Look away, wait for the slight pin prick and try not to think of your blood in a syringe. No problem. ECG scan; not so easy. It turns out that to add to the list of things my moisturising cream effectively deters (dry skin (obviously) and more strangely, mosquitoes,) I can add electrodes. To begin with the one under my arm clung on for as long as it could - about 3 seconds - before dropping off. My nurse patiently patted it back in place. It then fell off again about 5 seconds later. My nurse patiently patted it back in place again. It then fell off again, immediately, in perfect tandem with the one under my other arm. My nurse, not so patiently, stuck them both back on, again. They all stayed in place for about 30 seconds. Then the two on my chest slipped off and one second later so did the one under my ribs which had behaved this far. My nurse's patience was waning fast. She was no longer patting anything, more slapping wildly and indiscriminately at my bare chest. I didn't know where to look so I just shut my eyes. Finally, after well over 10 minutes, electrodes and skin had been tamed long enough to get the job done. Slight problem being that while my nurse was playing 'whack-a-mole' on my naked upper torso, I had been holding my breath in the vain attempt not to move a single muscle. The electrical activity of my heart had probably stopped a long time ago.

This is funny for another reason. In my previous life my job was to procure medical goods for the NHS. One of the contracts I was responsible for was ECG electrodes. The NHS spends over £28m a year on these things and in my view this is far too much. I had told the CEO of the leading manufacturer of these products as much on a number of occasions. I have no doubt that this gentleman had cared dearly about providing high quality, reasonably priced electrodes to the NHS once upon a time. Now, however, having just sold his company for a lot of money, he had more than one eye on his condo in the Caribbean. In our protracted negotiations I wanted him to reduce his prices for the new contract. He did not. His reason was simple and I kid you not; his products had 'superior sticking' power to his branded rivals. Yes! I had the bastard! First hand evidence right under my nose. I looked down to read the name on the electrode clinging on nearest to my armpit. Damn! These weren't his bloody brand!

Chapter 13.

Stuart Little and Big John

One of the disadvantages of being off work is that you enter the 'tradesman trap'. Full time workers simply do not understand how lucky they are in successfully avoiding this treacherous world. This week I have been told my drains need upgrading, my loft requires twenty first century lagging and I could benefit from a spot of herringbone landscaping to my driveway. Or possibly; I don't.

I have also finally been caught by Stuart 'Little'. Stuart is our window cleaner. 'Little' because he really is extremely little - which I find funny, and little because this is how much I have paid him so far. Well, actually nothing is more accurate. The reason I haven't paid him is because Stuart (this is actually his name) is a bloody awful window cleaner. I owe him £32 for four window cleans. I am not paying. I am not paying because my windows are not clean. This is actually not true. My windows were clean before Stuart came along. They are now 'smeary' on a cloudy day and veritably opaque when the sun comes out. This is because Stuart's 'big idea' is to do away with the conventional ladder and replace it with an extremely long brush handle; nothing wrong with this concept except that he has also done away with soap and water. I should have seen the warning signs when Stuart proudly announced after completing his first 'clean' that, "You may find your windows will be smeary (SMEARY???) the first few times as it is a new 'system' we are using and it takes the windows a few times to adjust." Yes, a bloody system that doesn't clean windows! The actual Stuart Little could do a better job with a really tiny ladder and shammy leather all of his own. What kind of statement is that? Can you imagine going to a restaurant and the waiter saying, "Sorry, but you may find your first few meals with us bloody awful; it is just that our ovens are taking time to adjust!" It has not exactly got the ring of a successful business empire to me. Anyway, next Tuesday I will make a point of being out when Stuart Little is about.

The second trade I have time to observe is the wicked under-word of mobile ice cream procurement. In the same way as clowns freak me out, I have never been entirely comfortable with ice-cream men and ours is called 'Big John' for Christ's sake. You do not mess with Big John on any level. If he says he is out of magnums, then he is out of magnums. No questions asked. What all of us come to realise upon observing this business is that it is no happy chance encounter that the ice-cream man, with his merry tinkling bell, has magically stopped outside YOUR house just at the point when you feel peckish for your pudding. No, we know the truth. It is down to calculated, strategic, mafia-esque planning. The problem being that once your house has been 'targeted' Big John will be there without fail every single night; waiting. And he will wait. And wait. And wait. Until you break and tearfully ask for a Mr Whippy with all the trimmings. But I have been strong. It has taken over three weeks of stand-off. But finally at 4.30 every evening Big John drives slowly past our house without stopping. We are free.

Chapter 14.

Sudoku and the Surprise Nipple

As I speak to friends and family about my experiences I am gathering some great and strange stories about prosthetic breasts and daytime gym antics. Here are the best;

1. One friend witnessed a lady cycling while making a beaded necklace. I actually misheard her and thought she had said bearded necklace, which conjured up an altogether different image to be honest.
2. Another friend saw a lady cycling while knitting. Apparently she had her pink ball of wool nestling nicely in the drink bottle holder of her bike; brilliant. All she was missing was a steaming hot cuppa and Corry on the big screen.
3. Another choice curio was the man completing the Sudoku while on the running machine. I initially, and wrongly, presumed that this was the paper version of the puzzle but apparently, and unbeknown to me all the machines at my gym have inbuilt pre-programmed puzzles. Who knew? Curious, I checked them out today and low and behold, under the more conventional options of TV and radio sits 'Games'. Press this button and you are presented with a veritable smorgasbord of puzzles; Sudoku, Patience, Backgammon, Mah-jong. All these years, why was this not part of my gym initiation? I love puzzles! I love running! I am sold.

And so to the gathering prosthetic/ reconstructed breast stories; loads to choose from but the best two for me are:

1. Friends of the family were on holiday in Tenerife and enjoying a swim in the sea. Those who are familiar with this stretch of the Atlantic coast will know that the seas off Tenerife are not for the faint hearted, or probably, in hindsight, the prosthetic breasted. Safe to say, post a particularly mighty wave, the brave and amazing lady who is the centre of this story, felt her prosthetic breast make a break for freedom and launch itself into the breakers. Her and her family then had to spend a frantic 15 minutes searching amongst the innocent bathers as her 'prosthy' bobbed joyfully amongst the waves. I love to imagine the moment when 'Linda' (let's call her that for alliteration sake) lazily lolling her left leg in the water from her lilo, just catches out of the corner of her eye what looks suspiciously like a Portuguese man o' war menacingly making its way towards her. She is out of there!

2. The second tale is about a marvellous and genuine Lancashire lady who works for a friend of the family. On all accounts, she is not backwards in coming forward in talking about what she has been through. The story goes she was talking to her boss a few weeks ago and he was enquiring politely as to how she was and what she was planning for Xmas and what she was particularly looking forward to. To which she replied, straight up; "Well, now that you ask, I actually can't wait for Xmas 'cos I've decided to treat myself. I'm

going to buy myself a brand new nipple." Utterly brilliant, her poor boss did not know what to say to this, obviously. He probably, even now is still waking in the dead of night in a cold sweat from his recurring dream of Xmas Day. Picture it. A huge ornately gift-wrapped present box gradually makes its way to his out stretched hands. You know you want it! It's for me? Really? Yes! Open it! Open it, open it! Is it a new camera? A new iPad? Er, no.

Chapter 15.

Up to see 'R 'Enry

Today is a beautiful early autumn day so I made the most of it and went to the Henry Moore Sculpture Park, in West Bretton, Wakefield. I love this park for a number of reasons and enjoy walking round its grounds with my family. I have to admit, I had never really been a massive fan of Henry Moore's Sculptures. I don't know whether I had just seen too many of them in ugly town centres, but his saggy bottomed women with their unfinished little Modigliani heads left me a bit cold. However, the recent fantastic exhibition of his sculptures and drawings here over the last few months has changed my mind. Paying proper attention to what he was trying to do and seeing that his inspiration was coming from places he loved like Brimham Rock and Flamborough Head, I got it. Stand in front of one of his more abstract sculptures then walk very slowly round it and you will see what I mean. It changes shape, it is magical. There is another less high-brow reason why I have warmed to his women of late. Take a closer look; most of them have one, none, or nothing, where their breasts should be! Hoorah! Sculptural solidarity. I love it.

A lovely morning was topped off in style by the hour I spent having my lunch sitting in the sunshine with my two new octogenarian female friends. I believe only in the beautiful and singular county of Yorkshire could such a lunch take place. The sun is shining so everyone is sat outside of the parks cafe. I am sitting on a bench happy with my company only to be joined by two ladies who I can only politely describe as 'Yorkshire Characters'. Meet Rita Overend (aged 84) and Nelly Wold (aged 83). I kid you not. And how do I know their full names and ages? Because they told me; they also told me the full names and ages of their 8 children, the full names and ages of their twelve grandchildren and the full names and ages of their late husbands and their respective family members. They also told me why they liked Wakefield (close by) and don't like Pontefract (too far). Why they like 'Strictly' (that Winkleman women) and don't like 'Bake Off' (that Hollywood character). Why they like Rugby League (our boys) and don't like Union (those posh boys). And why they are looking forward to this afternoon (cuppa, then supper, then a flutter????) And so on and so on and so on...

And why did they both like coming to the Sculpture Park? Well, as Nelly put it, "Aye, we like 't' come up 't' see 'r' 'Enry' whenever our legs let us, don't we Rita? It's nice 'n' quiet and peaceful." PEACEFUL???

Chapter 16.

Flat Packed Failure

Today I have mostly not been building the flat packed bed for the spare room. This is because flat packed furniture and I don't like each other very much. Depressingly, it's likely over the next few months that a spare bed is going to be required and our current one has given up the ghost. I have plenty of bad experiences of building this stuff but probably the most painful is 'The Cot.'

In my defence, remember, I was full term pregnant, huge, and prone to acute bouts of over-heating and suffering from a mild case of narcolepsy. I should have seen the warning signs. The assembly instructions strangely seemed to be written on ancient parchment and on closer inspection they appeared to be hieroglyphics. The first page looked like an origami swan then there was an arrow pointing to page two which was a picture of an immaculate cot. So I did what I always do. Screw the instructions; I would go with my gut. How hard can it be? There are only 5 pieces to this thing. Front, back bottom, sides x 2. Let's go.

Forty minutes, later, with only a light sweat on, I have the right side ready to slot into place to complete the job. Hang on. Why isn't it going in? Jesus. The front and the back boards LOOKED exactly the same, except for TWO TINY little holes needed to enable the right side to slide up and down. Okay. I'll just switch them round, no problem. Yes, problem. You can't just 'switch' them round. Time to disassemble; we can do this. Let's go again.

Fifty minutes later, and only one small kip on the floor, I am ready to slip the final sliding side in once again. Jesus Christ! You have got to be joking me! The end panel was correct this time but I had assembled it the wrong way round! Just one TINY arrow sticker would have been all it took to help me out here. MANUFACTURER!!! COME ON!!! Again, no easy flipping of the side panel. TIME TO DISASSEMBLE a second time. This could break a woman.

One reviving Guinness, a secret sob and a sweat drenched maternity top later, I was finally victorious. I gathered my family around me to show them the results of my hard labour. Impressed? My husband smiled weakly, and said, "It's a great job, sweet, but why have you built it in the spare room when it needs to be in the nursery."

DISASSEMBLE!!!

Chapter 17.

Playing the 'C' card

In the same way as stating, "I'm with Clooney, you know," probably ups your chances of getting a table at the Ivy, it appears that letting certain people know that "I'm with cancer" has leverage. Sadly, the 'Cancer Card' can get you places. Apologies if this offends, but it is the truth and I have evidence.

The receptionist at my private eye-clinic has made it her life work over the last two years to make it as difficult as possible for me to see my doctor at a date and time that is convenient for me. Dr Chung, according to his receptionist, does not have a clinic on Monday afternoons, Tuesdays, Wednesdays, Thursday or Fridays. His Monday morning clinic also only takes place if it was a full moon the previous evening, it's a leap year, the month ends in 'er' and Dr Chung is in the mood.

It was time. I'm not proud but it had to be done. I needed an appointment before my op on the 22nd what choice did I have. Sod it, let the bitch really work; I lied and said my op was this coming Thursday to really stick it up her. "Oh" she said curtly, "I will see what I can do and I will ring you back." Now, unless she had actually been sitting on Dr Chung's lap during our conversation, there was no way in the 45 seconds it took her to ring me back she had put the phone down, rung Mr Chung, explained the situation and rung me back. I was on to her. "Hi, is that Lucy? Yes, we can fit you in on Monday at 2.30." I thought you might. I could have fun with this.

The 'C'card' can also be used by proxy. A colleague of Tom's (yes, you know who you are) has, over the years, nurtured a long and creative list of excuses for his wife, as to why he is home from work late (A.K.A in the pub for a few swift ones). She knows that he knows that she knows where he really is. I think his role is just to keep the invented excuses (i.e. lies) fresh. So it's good news that he now has a new one to add to is oeuvre, given the fact that he has "just been celebrating Tom's 30th," for the last 13 years. So all is good, as from now on he is understandably going to be late home as he has been, "talking to Tom about Lucy". The fact that I haven't even been mentioned between the pints of Silver King is not the point. I am a staunch believer in the importance of beer and conversation amongst friends and colleagues to ease the pain of the working week. I am just happy that I can be of help.

Chapter 18

I Didn't Know You Played?

I am learning to play the guitar. Technically I should have LEARNT to play the guitar by now. I am not sure what the watershed is between learning and learnt but I fear it's sooner than six years. Anyway, safe to say Eric has not been on the phone yet. And now I have no excuse as work is not in the way of practice time. I have always wanted to play the guitar for the same reasons as we all pick up things past puberty – to impress.

Those who know me well will know that I am a skilled dreamer. My dreams are brilliant. All my dreams have one recurring theme. In them I am amazing (what? they're my bloody dreams). My absolute favourite is the "Wow, I didn't know you played the guitar!" dream. Just pipped for the primary slot are, "The one where I win Olympic Gymnastics Gold' – my vault scores straight 10's every time", and the "The one where I play centre for Wakefield Wildcats" – I score the winning try under the sticks in the Challenge Cup Final (lots of suspension of disbelief required here obviously, it being Wakefield I am playing for).

"The One where I play the guitar" is my favourite, though. Of course there is a camp fire, a warm, late evening beach. There's beer, (etc.) and of course beautiful people, sitting around sharing their innermost secrets. And there is music. Someone starts to sing, they have a stunning voice, of course. And then there is a guitar. Don't ask me where it comes from it just appears every time. "Can anyone play?" Oh yes, I can play. And boy, can I play. I break their hearts. My portfolio is massive. I can play anything; blues, jazz, folk, pop. They fall in love with me, boys and girls, both. I can even hear someone crying. It's beautiful. The sun slowly sets; nobody wants to go home. I end with Wonderful Tonight. It is wonderful. I am wonderful.

Back to the real world. I started with lessons in a group tutorial. The first week there were twenty of us, by the 5th week there were nine of us left. We could be broken down into three groups. The under 14's whose super absorbent brains and agile figures could strum a suspended F minor chord for three hours non-stop without getting rigor-mortis. Nirvana, Paramore and Death Cab for Cutie were their artistic idols. Safe to say I was not in this group. The second group was the Cool Dads who were pretending they were beginners but had actually been trying to learn on and off for the last forty years. Getting to play second guitar in their local Squeeze tribute band was their goal. And then there was me, the mid-life acoustic loving dreamer; the genuine beginner who just really wanted to be Joni Mitchell's and Nick Drake's love child.

After nearly giving up after a particularly soul-destroying group rendition of Green Days, Boulevard of Broken Dreams, the chord progression of which meant I couldn't hold a toothbrush for a week, I did begin to get the hang of it. I can now play at least fifteen minutes' worth of other people's music with a passable singing voice to go alongside. I don't get any more public than drunken friends and I can't see any imminent late night beach party debuts but it's great to have more time to strum. And dream.

Chapter 19.

Flash Dance Fantasy

I am having my hair cut short today. From shoulder length to above the ears in one fell swoop. I am even going in with a picture. I don't look anything like the lady in the picture and she doesn't look anything like me and I still won't look anything like her afterwards, I don't doubt. However, given the fact my lovely and talented hairdresser has cut my hair exactly the same way for the last 10 years, I am thinking she may need at least a little guidance. I am looking forward to it. It's time for a change anyway.

The last time I went to the hairdressers with a fantasy picture was 1983. I wanted to look like Alexandra Owens from Flash Dance, the movie. I didn't end up looking anything like her either. Actually on reflection that was probably a good thing. The cropped look then was in a vain attempt to be noticed by the luscious Simon Jones. It didn't work. This time it's to create an easy step one from lots of locks to not so many locks.

I like my hairdressers for a number of reasons. It is often a very funny and genuine place to spend a few hours and a great opportunity to read some really trashy gossip magazines while the dye turns back the years. There is, however, another reason why I like my hairdressers. It is called Charlie's. It is called Charlie's for the honest and straightforward reason that it's owned by Charlie. This is very unusual. It has always troubled me as to why, uniquely, hairdressing salons feel the urge to give themselves such stupid and monumentally unfunny 'pun' names. Over the years I have had my hair cut at Sheerlocks (get it?), A Cut Ahead (not funny and not clever), Shear-N-Dipity (just, no), Cuts Both Ways, Eticut and the Mane Attraction. To put this into perspective, if your local butcher decided to team up with your local greengrocer and proudly renamed themselves "Your Local Meat and Two Veg," you would be absolutely outraged. You would probably march right in there and demand to know what on earth they were playing at. Quite right. However, I bet most people wouldn't have the slightest problem nipping in to their local 'Short 'n' Curlies' for a quick cut and blow would they?

Chapter 20.

Two Negatives Make a Positive

I went to Emily's parent's evening last night. It was lovely to hear such positive comments about my daughter. She is extremely lucky to be in a school that takes so much time to understand and nurture its pupils.

The standout comment about Emily of the evening, however, came from her top set maths teacher. These were her words;

"Emily has been rather outraged by negative numbers this term."

Superb. That's my girl. I am totally with her on this one. It immediately took me back to when I was 11 and my love affair with maths came to an abrupt end at exactly the same point.

Up until first term Senior School I thought maths was brilliant. Basically maths was about memory, repetition and competitiveness. Everything was a test and I loved tests. One teacher, I remember, used to set weekly times table tests; the winner of which was awarded a glorious, glossy A2 Star Wars Poster. By the end of the year I had over 30 of the bloody things. I had no interest in Star Wars whatsoever, but I loved these posters; they were material evidence of my mathematical genius. And then it happened.

"This week, class, we are going to learn about negative numbers." The fog descended. Minus 6 plus 5 is minus 1. WHAT? WHY? Two minuses equal a plus. THAT'S JUST NONSENSE! And it gets worse. Two minuses might make a plus but two plusses don't make a minus and a minus and a plus still make a minus!!!! Well, I had been sold a total lie. All those years in the happy, positive world, where the plus sign is king and all things stop sensibly and finitely at zero, and nobody had bothered to tell me about the dark side where negatives were more powerful than positives. Actually, thinking about it, maybe my primary school teacher was trying to let us know about the black abyss that was out there with those portentous Star Wars posters.

Negative numbers marked the end of my love affair with maths. And perhaps the sadness and frustration I felt was more than dumbness. Perhaps this world of negativity worried me because, let's be honest, for most of us who don't go on to do maths 'A' level and the jam subjects of further, further and further maths; (I don't remember being given the opportunity to study further geography) maths, in our later life is basically personal and/ or professional finance, and for most of us it predominantly sits in the negative. Mortgages. Debt. Overdrafts. Negative equity. Underperforming business plans, blah, blah, blah. We are all fully aware of the capitalist game we have to play but in moments of clarity it still bothers us like it bothered me when I was 11. It bothered me twenty years later too. I remember my first annual mortgage statement from the bank; it read as follows;

Dear Sucker,

Thank you so much for working your ass off every month to pay off your monumental debt to us that we are enjoying repackaging and selling for our profit and gain. As you will see from the table above, this has had fuck all impact over the last 12 months on the amount of money you still owe us. In fact, you have really done no more than licked the edges of the interest that we are charging you each month. You will see that you now owe us exactly the same amount that you owed us at the beginning of the year. This will be the case for at least the next 25 years.
Have a nice day.

Compare this to my Gran's reaction, about the time I was eleven, when she discovered to her horror that the TV shop wanted to sell her a new video player on an HP deal. She was outraged and could not get her head around how anybody would want to purchase something with someone else's money and it wasn't called stealing. The video player was £45.

My daughter doesn't really understand this wicked world yet. As long as the bank of Mum and Dad has the readies to exchange for toys and books, all is good. This term, however, she has had to dip her toe into it, and her reaction seemingly was the same as mine. I quickly retracted my toe and skipped happily off to the wonderful world of the arts. There are no negative numbers lurking in Art and Literature. I suspect my daughter will do the same.

Chapter 21.

Boiling Point

Over the last 25 years of our relationship, myself and Tom haven't really fallen out over anything much. The most pissed we can get with each other is no more than, **him**; my zealousness for over tidying, **me**; his inability to put the lid back properly on anything. That's it, really; until now. Something, or rather, I like to believe 'someone' has come between us and her name is THE BOILER.

She has been a growing problem in our relationship for the last 4 and half years but it has now reached boiling point - or rather it hasn't reached boiling point - which is the problem. Like many domestic appliances she won't make it easy for us and just pack it in. That would be far too easy. She likes to live in the appliance twilight zone between working perfectly some of the time and not working at all most of the time, and frequently just about working with a hint of about to not work. We are kept on morning and nightly tenterhooks as to whether she can be asked to provide us with any twentieth century hot water and then find ourselves strangely thanking her when she condescends to do so. I hate her.

This morning she orchestrated the usual scenario. Shower time. No hot water. "I'll sort it" I bravely offer. Right, you cow, I'll show you. 'Showing her' is, however, easier said than done. Firstly, she lives under the stairs. Secondly, she nestles inconveniently behind the washing machine and finally she lives in pitch black darkness. 'Sorting her' involves having to climb, belly down, onto the washing machine, and donning a pose somewhere between a Chaturanga Dandasanga and a Downward Dog, with a torch in one hand, while the other hand blindly tries to fiddle with her dial-y things. The infinitely specific position each of these dials MUST be in for her to respond, I am convinced is different every morning. Safe to say after 15 minutes of fumbling she remains stony white faced and unresponsive to my touch. Nothing; cold and silent, every time.

"You're doing it wrong" says Tom. "Step aside". Here we go again, I can't even watch this. He deftly climbs aboard the washing machine, dons the torch like a pro, starts to whisper sweet nothings to her, and after no more than 10 minutes of softly caressing her dials, she is hot and purring perfectly. Well, I know exactly what is going on here and I am not happy. I'll take your hot water this morning, missy, but I know what you are up to.

I believe she is waiting you see; waiting for her final revenge. She is waiting until I am weak. It will be February; at least minus twelve degrees outside. It will definitely be a Sunday. I will be post op and chemo fuddled and Tom will probably be out and I will need hot water. Then she will finally have her moment. Well, I am on to her. I have her number - well I have the number of a plumber – because she has got to go.

Chapter 22.

Going Turbo

I have just been informed that my new car will be ready at the end of the month. I don't need a new car really. My middle management, mass produced motor is in as mint condition as the day I got it four years ago. But it is a company car and the deal is you rent it and then trade up when its time is up. The problem is I am very aware of the fine line between the understated 'nice car' and the overstated 'nob car'. I fear I have crossed the line. My current cars' only special effect is to cut out when stationary to save on emissions. This can be disconcerting but the worst that happens is you get confused and don't move anywhere at the lights. No damage done. My new car, however, has a few more and darker talents. I have in a weak moment gone for the 'Sports Package'. It has a turbo boost button for starters. One thing I don't need in my life right now is a turbo button. 'Going turbo' has cost me licence points up to the high teens, back down again, and up again a few times over. Don't get me wrong, this is no DB7, I don't get a passenger ejector seat and missile launchers out front, but when it 'goes turbo', it's scary. For a start the screen lights up on the dash board with a skeletal image of the car with all the engine parts that have now kicked in, glowing dangerously red and you immediately can't help channelling Jenson Button. It's a bit disconcerting really. Nought to 60 in 7 seconds and

I'm going to be wearing a fucking wig. It's too incongruous for words. I would love this car to meet my first car. It would be an interesting sight. My first car was a beautiful bright orange mini. On the outside this car did a pretty good job of pretending to be a car. On the inside it was fooling nobody. Firstly, the steering wheel only intermittently connected with the wheel axis; secondly, in order to change gear you had to pump the clutch up and down as if you were pumping up a paddling pool with one of those ineffective manual inflators. Driving this thing was exhausting. No surprises that eventually, while trying to coerce it into second gear round a tight bend my foot went clean though the floor. This thing was a death trap. It was only one step away from a bloody pedal car. Amazingly, my Dad managed to sell it to a chap who said he was "only going to drive it at night" – to avoid tax or insurance no doubt. There is no way this guy is still living.

Out of body experiences with cars have happened to me a few times. The worst one was a few years ago with a car I bought from my Dad. Parking up after a long and frustratingly sedentary day at a conference in Harrogate, I couldn't get out of the thing quickly enough in order to go for a life returning run after work. Where we lived, private parking was a challenge at best so I used to just park up on the road. So this is what I did. On my return from my refreshing run, Tom was home and he looked concerned. "Sit down", he said, sternly. So I did. "You have crashed the car". Now, when someone else informs you that YOU have crashed the car because you weren't aware that you had crashed the car, then you know that something truly tragic has taken place. And it had. I had single-handedly managed to crash the car while being out for a run. It appears that the checklist of, 'parking on a hill? Check. Hand break on? Check. Into gear? Check; had escaped me on this occasion. Consequently, my lovely new car had rolled itself sedately across the road, gathering speed as it eased itself down the hill, before crumpling heroically into our neighbour's wrought iron gate. Impressively, (although I couldn't bring myself to see the evidence) the engineering of a wrought iron gate turned out to be vastly superior to that of a 4-year old Peugeot. My car had collapsed pathetically. The gate had merely caved in a little. Luckily my lovely neighbour had a sense of humour and a tractor. The former meant he was happy to settle for a 70 quid pacifier and the latter meant my devastated car got air lifted off the gate to the knackers' yard. Safe to say now I only park on flat ground, always leave the car in gear, triple check the hand break is on and scout the landscape for wrought iron fences. Actually, thinking about it, I should have opted for a 'parking package' with my new car not a 'sports package'. Damn.

Chapter 23.

Hampered

In a few days' time, I am going to be hampered. I am prepared for it. As the verb goes I will be hindered, held back, impeded. Not today though. Today I have been happily hampered, big style, by my wonderful, amazing work colleagues. A wicker basket of wonders sits on my kitchen table. I am seriously touched. I am seriously touched because this is no ordinary hamper. This is a hamper of love. I will tell you why. Below is a list of what is in my hamper:

Colouring book and pencil crayons (I do my daughter's colouring homework for God's sake. I love colouring in that much!)
Chocolates (the non-fancy good and proper milk chocolate kind)
Books about adventures (yes!)
Socks (the very warm and especially woolly kind)

Jam (all favourite fruits and no marmalade (the devils jam)
Bottles of beer (light and hoppy - again my favourite)
Packets of fruit and nuts (healthy but never seem it)
Crackers (I bloody love crackers)
Sweets (pink marshmallows - nothing is superior)

Dry shampoo (possibly the greatest invention of the last decade)
Pure wool blanket (I am a softy at heart)
Scented candle (seriously posh – Jo Malone no less)

Below is a list of my absolute favourite things in this world:
Colouring books and pencil crayons (I do my daughter's colouring homework for God's sake I love colouring in that much!)
Chocolates (the non-fancy good and proper milk chocolate kind)
Books about adventures (yes!)
Socks (the very warm and especially woolly kind)
Jam (all favourite fruits and no marmalade (the devils jam)
Bottles of beer (light and hoppy – the best kind)
Packets of fruit and nuts (healthy but never seem it)
Crackers (I bloody love crackers)
Sweets (marshmallows – nothing is superior)
Dry shampoo (possibly the greatest invention of the last decade)
Pure wool blanket (I am a softy at heart)
Scented candle (seriously posh – Jo Malone no less)

I have to be honest about hampers received hitherto in my life. There have been three kinds;

1) The hamper that is actually nine tenths shredded paper and only one tenth present.
2) The hamper that is packed full of goodies that you don't really want.
3) The hamper that is packed full of goodies that the person who sent you the hamper really wants.

This hamper is none of the above. The only issue I have with my hamper is that it is not quite big enough for me to climb inside, shut the lid and hide away amongst my favourite things. I could nestle up in my lovely soft pure wool blanket, munch away contently on my Percy Pig Marshmallows and immerse myself in Jon Krakauer's 'Thin Air' by the light of my Jo Malone. Someone come and get me out when Thursday comes. Or actually, don't.

Chapter 24.

My! What lovely long eyelashes you have!

"And such a pretty little face!" These were the complimentary last words I heard from the theatre doctors before my lights went out. Why, thank you very much. I went to sleep happy and woke up a few hours later ever happier; euphoric even, to be honest. Relieved it was over and a bit amazed that I felt ok. I even had an immediate quick peek at the scar. Strangely, the first word that came to mind was funky; a big serious black line through breast cancer. Good. A quick check to make sure I knew who I was and I was out of recovery and onto the ward. I would have my bags packed and be home tomorrow.

One heroic faint in the ladies' toilet, a mild midnight hypo and two melon sized hematomas' later and I was not feeling quite so chipper! (A common and not serious complication from such surgery apparently.) But very unfortunate and very painful. I now had an unwanted second date with my surgeon to sort it out. Same place same time, 24 hours after my first one. Not ideal. Two doses of an aesthetic in as many days and it is safe to say I didn't wake up quite so chipper the second time. Plus I don't remember any one complimenting on my eyelashes this time.

But I am home now and have had the best roast chicken dinner of my life and the best porridge breakfast of my life, and cushioned between these, the best 16 hours kip of my life. Oh, and easily the best ginger cake of my life, baked and dropped off by lovely, caring friends.

If you are unlucky enough to stay in hospital for three nights and four days, it is safe to say it will be an education. I have learnt some things I didn't know and didn't want to know, and a few more things I didn't know but am glad I now know. Here are a few of them:

1. **Anaesthetists, without exception, have zero people skills.**

I have concluded that this may be because they are not actually human. I think, in fact, they might all be manufactured in a secret factory somewhere in deepest Swindon. Both mine barged into the arena, clearly to the consternation of the doctors and nurses, who were already in conversation with me, in order to gather the specific facts that they needed. Any dental work? Any metal work? Any piercings? The funniest moment was when my second anaesthetist couldn't find a way in through my drawn cubicle curtain. Honestly, it had to be seen to be believed. It took him well over 3 minutes to negotiate his way in; at one point he had wrapped himself entirely in the thing. This man had the brilliance and skill to put me to safe and painless sleep during unsafe and painful surgery and the fucker couldn't even negotiate the opening in a bloody curtain. Brilliant.

2. **There are two types of nurses.**

The soft, warm handed, kind-hearted nurses that don't hurt you and ask about why you're here, but then disturbingly leave you slightly and annoyingly inconvenienced afterwards. Your panic buzzer frustratingly just out of reach, your gown uncomfortably up your bum, your water jug insultingly inches out of reach. Then there are the stern, non-smiling, cold handed, slightly frightening nurses that you suspect think you need to be shown a little bit of pain for your own good. However, these nurses are off the scale efficient and leave you relieved and in utter comfort without you even noticing how on earth they have achieved it. On reflection I think I prefer 'stern nursie'.

3. **Every ward has an interminably nosey patient.**

Just like every street has one, every ward has a 'Sheila from South Barnsley'. (All names changed for patient confidentiality purposes, obviously.)
Aaaah, 'Our Sheila'. Age: 67. Length of time in hospital: weeks and weeks. Ailment: yet to be diagnosed. This, I am afraid to say is because I suspect there was nothing bloody wrong with her. She just loved being in hospital. And she took her job as professional nosey parker extremely seriously. She had a number of very important jobs. Primary amongst these was to keep her encyclopaedic knowledge of all patients current, past, and potential future ailments, together with a detailed past personal history, on this ward and all 13 of the

hospitals other wards, as up to date as it was humanly possible for one lady while being in bed. She achieved this by perching, Mary Poppins-like on the edge of her bed, her neck strained and her ears alert to absolutely everything that was being said. Remember, curtains are not sound proof. This woman knew everything. Her second job was to ensure that everybody else was kept abreast of all this information, whether they wanted to hear it or not.

Sheila's second most important job was to point out the bloody obvious. A few examples: the wind blows loudly outside, cue Sheila, "ooh, it's windy outside." The tea trolley arrives; cue Sheila, "ooh, tea's up." Lights go out, cue Sheila, "lights out, ladies!" Give me strength. Sheila's third important job was to eat. I have never witnessed anything like it in my life. Remember, the biggest cardiovascular exercise any of us were taking was to shuffle five paces to the loo. This is an inventory of a typical day's consumption:

Breakfast: 4 pieces of toast, two brown, two white, butter, no jam.
Cup of tea: white, 3 sugars, 3 biscuits
Lunch: tomato soup, roast chicken dinner, lemon gateau, cheese and biscuits
Cup of tea: white, 3 sugars, 3 biscuits
Dinner: Minestrone soup, roast beef dinner, apple pie and custard, cheese and biscuits.

If you think the NHS is in so much budgetary trouble because of an ageing population, government cuts and the rising cost of care, think again; it's the cost of keeping 'Our Sheila from South Barnsley' well fed.

Beyond her three key jobs, Sheila also delegated herself to an additional assignment during my stay; to be chief interpreter to the amazing 94-year old Elsie in the bed next to her. Elsie had taken a tumble in IKEA. Elsie was quite simply an incredible lady who had seen and done it all. Her only mistake in life to date was to take a tumble in IKEA and land herself in a hospital bed next to Sheila. Elsie being hard of hearing was enough of an excuse for Sheila to believe she needed to repeat everything, VERY LOUDLY that was said to Sheila and strangely also everything VERY LOUDLY that Elsie said back as if she believed deafness was actually contagious.

These were Sheila's day jobs; her night time job was to keep me awake with her monumental snoring. Sheila had operatic skills in this department. She led her little orchestra of female snorers every night with the acoustic might of Pavarotti. The only time she stopped was when her epiglottal reverberations reached such a pitch that she woke herself up. Accompanying Sheila nightly was the lady in the bed to my right. Her snoring was more of a jazz riff. She never found a rhythm but would then just go off score and improvise with noises I have never heard before in my entire life, or ever want to hear again. She was the Thelonius Monk of snoring. And finally, percussion was provided by the flatulent lady to my right. Enough said. Curtains came up on this nightly performance around 8.30pm and the final encore kicked in around 7.30am. My family know that I don't exactly weigh in as a light sleeper; I am more of a featherweight sleeper. If a neighbour eight doors down goes for a pee in the night I will not sleep through it. However, I would honestly challenge the deepest sleeper in South Barnsley to kip through what I was being subjected to. And finally to add insult to genuine injury, the highlight of the morning was Sheila waking from her sound snoring slumber to declare, "Ooh, another rough night for me!" If I had had to stay in for another night I may have been guilty of giving our Sheila a real reason to be in hospital!

4. Hospital visiting rules are there to be broken

Most patients understand that the 2 hour/two visitors to a bed rule is there for a reason. The lady to my right, however, believed the rules simply did not apply to her. At 6 o'clock more friends and family arrived to see her than I had at my bloody wedding. At one point at least four of them were virtually sitting on my bed due to the lack of space for her party. They proceeded to unpack what smelt like a Chicken Korma and the contents of at least three suitcases of goodies. When the bell went it appeared that they all dutifully left but I knew, because I could see and hear, that at least four of them had hidden out of sight under her bed and were heard to be whispering and sipping Indian Pale Ale until late in the evening, until they were discovered and given their marching orders by a less than impressed Sister.

5. Pain Management

It turns out that my perception of pain management is about 100 years out of date. Maybe this is due to too many trips to the Thackeray museum in Leeds where Emily and I used to dare to scare each other by watching the reconstructed film of the Victorian leg amputation. It turns out that surgery and pain management has moved on a bit since rusty saws and whisky soaked hankies between clenched teeth. Thank God. I have the energy of an iPhone battery and it feels like a baby elephant has taken up home on the right side of my chest but I am not in agony. Amongst the small pharmacy that I have started up by my bed I still have some serious manly, hard core, pain relief options available to me but at the moment, I am needing no more than girlie period pain, paracetamol. I have been flatteringly informed by the doctors that I have the pain threshold of a sumo wrestler and the resting heart beat of a professional athlete (48 bpm). Given the fact that going to the toilet is my greatest achievement today; however, I don't think either of these assigned skills will be required in the near future.

Chapter 25.

Drain Training

One of the joyous outcomes of a mastectomy is the fact you have to get used to being attached to a drain. Believe me, this sounds worse than it is but it remains a hindrance at best. This lovely piece of kit's job is obviously to drain away excess blood and fluid from the wound that would otherwise build up. Been there, done that, no thank you. It can only be described as a plastic hand grenade thingy attached to a long tube sown in to the side of me. Drain training involves being shown how to empty it so it keeps on sucking. Lovely. It's a bit like macabre paint balling really. The biggest problem, in actuality, is what to do with it when you are on the move (I use the word 'move' loosely) as it is no surprise that the major clothing chains have not taken it upon themselves to provide any fashionable attire that come with 'handy drain pockets'. I considered putting on my fishing waistcoat inside out and popping it in my fly pocket but thought against it at the last moment. Actually, Tom says it rather reminds him of a swim feeder that he has used to catch eels within the past. Late night fishing trip anyone?

Chapter 26.

Rabbit Ragu I love you

I've been thinking. I believe there is such a thing as 'the caring curve'.

At one end of this curve is abandonment. Not ideal. At the other end is claustrophobic molly coddling. No better, really. In the middle is the sweet spot; understanding, patience, premonition, selflessness, hardness. Safe to say Tom has hit the sweet spot. No surprises there.

Interestingly, there appears to be a corresponding care-ee curve. At one end is abject laziness; very tempting. At the other end is over zealous activity; a bit stupid. In the middle is the brave and sweet patient. I am trying my best to stay around this point:

"Tom, darling, when you have a second would you mind getting me another drink of water? Thank you so much."

"Tom, sweet, when you are free, would it be possible for you to get me the papers, the sport section, if you've read it of course. Thanks ever so much."

"Tom, honey, any chance, when you are finished with what you are doing you could possibly help me to the loo? You're a star, thanks, hon."

"Tom, babe, if it's not too much trouble would you mind getting my computer for me and plugging it in? Thanks, ever so much."

"Tom, is it ok if you leave me now as I think I need to rest up and have a little sleep. Thanks so much for looking after me."

But I am afraid to admit I have dipped into the odd bit of:

"Tom, get me a water top up will you?"

"Tom, can you get me the papers, sports section, ta."

"Tom, I need a hand to the loo, please."

"Tom, can you get my computer now, ta."

"Tom, you can go now, I need to sleep"

And worse, I am not proud to admit I have descended into a tiny bit of:

"Tom, I need water!"

"Tom, the papers, sports section!"

"Tom, the loo. Now!"

"Tom, computer, I need it!"

"Tom, fuck off, I'm tired."

And all the time Tom remains bang on the sweet spot!

There is, of course, another very important 'caring curve'. I have, in fact, been on this curve for the last 25 years. It is the 'carer cook curve' and Tom has been hitting the sweet spot for decades. In my view there are two reasons you need to eat. The more mundane of the two is for calorific content. If this is all that interests, you then good luck to you; eat whatever crap you like. Get full. Move on. Boring. Then there is the real reason to eat; the life enhancing, physical and emotional high of glorious cooking from the heart.

There are also two types of cooks. There is the monumental, occasional, show-off Saturday evening cook, whose meals end up posted on Face Book, God help us. With each locally sourced, pretentious ingredient catalogued for proud posterity. Safe to say Tuesdays frozen fish fingers and chips meal will not make it onto social media. Then there is the real, life-long, hard- core cook. The Monday night, school night, spring lamb and sweet peppers, cook. The Thursday night pork and apple, cook. The Sunday morning hangover bacon and fried eggs, cook. The calm and collected roast dinner for eight, cook. The slow roast neck of mutton stew, in the oven while we are in the pub, cook. The, in it for the long haul caring, cook. Tom has never so much as set foot in Face Book land so no prizes for guessing which kind of cook he is.

Since I have been out of hospital I have had succulent roast chicken. I didn't ask, but I know, it was fast cooked; then slow cooked in goose fat, with lovely new potatoes nestling by its side, sucking in the fatty juices while they roasted until their skins turned dark brown, thick and crispy. Pop them in your mouth whole and bite through the skin and the soft, creamy potato bursts out like eating a surprise, savoury fruit. Bloody wonderful.

I have had soft, succulent scallops almost hovering on the plate they were that perfect; plump amongst fluffy white rice and ginger and spring onions. Off the scale.

Tonight (because I like to know what's coming) we are having monkfish tails with chorizo sausage. Simply a match made in heaven.

And then, oh, and then. Then, we are having RABBIT RAGU. It is not possible to put into words what this dish does for me. I have an ever changing top ten 'favourite meals of my life' but nothing will ever knock my RABBIT RAGU off the premiere spot. Ever. It is not only about the considerable skill, time and effort that I know needs to go into the perfection of the dish, it is simply this; RABBIT RAGU quietly and perfectly says, I KNOW EVERYTHING ABOUT YOU AND I LOVE YOU.

Oh, and by the way, if you are waiting for an invite round for 'tea and sympathy', don't hold your breath as I am not sharing my RABBIT RAGU with anybody. Sorry.

Chapter 27.

Get down and give me seven shoulder shrugs

I am really loving the ITV series, SAS: Who Dares Wins. It's priceless entertainment. Usual format; somewhere in a secret location in the Welsh hills (why is it always a secret location in the Welsh hills?) a group of male contestants see whether they have what it takes (what do you think?) to become an SAS soldier by surviving the extremely tough and nasty recruitment process. My real reason for watching this programme (no doubt along with the majority of the female population) is to ogle at the ex-SAS soldiers that are putting the 'civilians' through their paces. If you are the kind of lady that is moved by a man with growling masculinity, piqued with genuine self-awareness, sensitivity and the ability to grow a full beard in an afternoon and pinch out the life of a man between his forefingers, then you will be moved. These are serious male specimens. Which is not what can be said for the pathetic pack of man boobed, pimply, blubbering numpties that are taking part in the process. Jesus, this lot wouldn't even make it onto a level 2 NVQ Apprenticeship in Sports Leadership at Wakefield College, never mind the bloody SAS. One special individual claimed he was, "a personal fitness instructor who loved dancing to Beyonce." Ok. Blubbering on his army bed upon been kicked out of the process, having shown absolutely zero characteristics of an SAS soldier, he sobbed, "I've never really been able to love myself." I think it's time to go home to Beyonce my friend.

And so to my tough and manly exercise regime. I have been charged with being 'up and about'. I have done the 'up' bit, which I take to mean not lying down and to include sitting as 'sitting up' not 'sitting down'. The 'about' bit I am not doing so well with. Plus, I have arm exercises to do. When I was given this glossy fold out map of minimal movement 'exercises' pre-op, I am ashamed to say I sniggered silently under my breath. Not now. I am not convinced by the cartoon lady in the pictures either. Firstly, she looks like Tintin's sister and not a day over 12. Despite the sympathetic lack of a right breast she looks fighting fit and finally she is wearing a tight red t-shirt. There is no way on earth, if she had been through what I have just been through, she would have got that thing on over her bloody head. My job is to follow this lovely cartoon lady (girl?) through two weeks of progressively 'tougher' arm and shoulder exercises. I am not on track. In fact, I am struggling with the warm up exercises which are no more than shoulder shrugs. I am proud to say I can do three tiny micro shoulder shrugs, not entirely apparent to the naked eye. I know where my shoulder is, obviously, because I can see it, but I can't quite locate the muscles to move it. The sensation is a bit akin to trying to wiggle your ears.

But I have been hanging on every word my lovely ex-SAS officers have had to say. They have told me again and again you much push yourself past what you think are your physical limits to find what you are truly capable of. I am pretty sure they weren't referring to tiny micro shoulder shrugs, but hey ho. Tomorrow I will push on bravely, past the pain barrier, for on day two I must graduate from shoulder shrugs to 'the back scratcher'. Come on, I can do this!

Chapter 28.

Weighty Tomes

I like to read fiction; a lot. I have inherited my love of fiction from my Mum; a lady who has written books full of the lists of the books that she has read. A woman who would think nothing of devouring a book in an afternoon; five in a week, at least twenty in a month and maybe two hundred plus in a year.

It is my Mum who has taught me the critical importance of having at least three books in reserve beyond the one in hand. Never; I mean, never be caught short when it comes to reading matter. There are simply no excuses.

Right now, though, I have a problem. It is not that I am short of reading matter. In fact, I have quite the opposite problem; I am in danger of being buried by my literary backlog. The problem is that my tomes are too weighty. I don't mean literarily weighty. They are – because they are predominantly Booker Prize short lists – very worthy and earnest – I mean they are literally as in, actually weighty. I am half way through 'A Little Life' by Hanya Yanagihara. An amazing book, but what was she thinking for Christ's Sake? Does she have no empathy? Its 720 pages long. I am literally crushed by it. Reading it is leisure and exercise rolled into one. I have to warm up before reading.

Someone once said to me, "You will never learn anything from reading fiction." Utter crap. I have a big opinion on this; here it is. The world is divided into those who take time to read fiction and those that poo poo it. If you are a poo poo-er you quite simply have NO IDEA what you are missing out on:

I read John Fowles, 'The Magus,' the story of Nicholas Urfe, a young British Graduate teaching on a small, very beautiful hot Greek island, while I was on holiday on a small very beautiful hot Spanish island. I didn't move for three days and can still remember now how outraged I was to be so manipulated by the author.

I read Barbara Kingsolver, 'The Lacuna', the epic journey from the Mexico City of artists Diego Rivera and Frida Kahlo to the America of Pearl Harbour, standing submerged all day in a warm swimming pool in the Tropical Riviera Mayo. When I finished the book fell apart, shrivelled and destroyed by the sun.

I bunked off school and hid under the duvet for four days to read J R R Tolkien's 'Lord of the Rings.' This was no 'Hobbit'. This was seriously scary shit. There was no time for school. The Black Riders still make we want to duvet dunk to this day.

I read Ian Rankin's, 'Freshmarket Close', in January, in freezing, hurricane ridden Edinburgh. Tucked up in bed, while the Victorian windows rattled and the crack addicts wailed below (no shit), willing Rebus to be rebellious.

I read Dickens 'Hard Times' while having a hard time in a God awful sweaty Oxford University student's room with zero oxygen and 100% sadness. Love Dickens to this day. Got to the end -of Dickens novels– not Oxford.

I read Gabriel Jose Garcia Marquez, 'Love in the Time of Cholera,' while falling in love and thinking I knew it all. I didn't.

I read Donna Tarts, 'The Goldfinch' while worrying about loss and how to care for the lonely. She didn't give me any answers.

I read Jonathan Franzen's, 'The Corrections' while trying to sum up the courage to change career. I am a wuss.

I read Caitlin Moran's, 'How to be a Woman' and split my sides with laughter over 'pubic trampolining.'

Yup, fiction is rubbish. It teaches you nothing. Thanks Mum.

Chapter 29.

Drain Free

I had my lovely drain removed yesterday; swiftly, professionally and sensitively by my hard core nurse. It is not a very pleasant procedure for a few reasons. Firstly, when the thing goes in its easy; you are off with the fairies. When it comes out, however, the fairies have fucked off and you are very much awake. Secondly, and inexplicably cruelly, the bit of the tube that is inside you is wider in circumference than the tube on the outside of you. What is all that about? Most procedures are given medical names. They tend to have the purpose of reassuring you of the technical/ medical skill required to carry them out. The technical term for removing a drain is, 'just pull'.

Being drain free kicks in the second stage of wound recovery. A house with no outside drains will flood if it rains. I am that house. Now that there is nowhere for my fluid to run to, it is happily flopping around in situ. Amazingly I appear to be naturally re-growing a cute double 'A' breast. I exaggerate. It is not that bad; half blown up saggy balloon, sort of describes it. Apparently this is normal as the community nurse has been out to visit me today. It is full blown up double 'F' party balloon that I should try and avoid. Apart from this very minor inconvenience I am feeling great and looking forward to a lovely (little) walk in the sunshine and burnt umber leaves this afternoon.

When, in a few more days, I fully engage with the outside world again, I will need to consider 'my look'. I have decided to flounce convention and instead of trying to trick the world into thinking I have a right breast, I am going to do the opposite and try and trick the world into thinking I don't have a left breast. I have a line in camisole boob tubes and gilets at the ready. Clever eh? I am going for the Kate Moss look. Obviously, not the legs, face, wardrobe or bank balance; just the flat chest. Amusingly, I have just read that to celebrate the supermodel's twenty-five years working in the fashion industry, Kate had Mayfair restaurant 34, model a champagne coupe on her left breast; vanity off the scale. Even more fascinating, this act has historical precedence as legend has it that the first champagne coupe that was made in the 18th century was modelled on Marie Antoinette's left breast. Brilliant. So, I have had a thought; what about the 'Lucy cut glass plate'? Why not? A handy place to keep your fruit or your bills, I'm not fussed. It could work. In fact, lets run with this, I could promote it internationally by modelling half naked on the front page of i-D style magazine (get it? . _) Kate Moss eat your heart out. No? A bit too risqué?

Chapter 30.

Not Kicking Leaves

It is a stunning, sunny Autumnal day today. Apparently the leaves are still on the trees and so spectacularly varied in colour this year due to the perfect combination of dryness, warmth and stillness. Various shades of red, yellow, purple, black, orange, pink, magenta, blue and brown. Pathetic fallacy for my arm pit to hip bruising!

It's a stunning day for another reason, as well; the list of things I can now do is ever so slightly longer than the list of things I can't do. Firstly, below is the ever diminishing list of the things I still can't do:

(Note: This list is limited to the things I still can't do that I COULD do before my op. For example, I still can't play the violin, but I couldn't play the violin before.)

1) Drive (who cares; walking should be made compulsory on days like this)
2) Shave my right arm pit (to be honest I can't even locate it at the moment so I don't really care)
3) Lift anything heavier than a small chopping board (we have a very big and heavy chopping board)
4) Clean (long may this continue)
5) Sneeze with confidence (nose holding is critical)

6) Hug (will be happy when I can do this again, I owe a few)
7) Play the piano, clarinet or piano (some would say no change there then)

Below, however, is the expanding list of things I can do:

1) Answer the door (only if it isn't locked.)
2) Shower solo (in sections and bottom half only.)
3) Turn the fire off (useless, because I can't actually turn it on.)
4) Ineffectual cleaning (just to annoy Tom.)
5) Shave my left armpit (it was getting French under there.)
6) Get up to Emily's attic room straight after getting up the stairs (with only a brief landing pause.)
7) Make myself tea and toast (essential).
8) Type (lying down is better than sitting up for some reason.)
9) Sleep on my left side (deliciously discovered early this morning.)
10) Iron one handed (not included as a household chore in my house.)

And finally:

11) Kick leaves (if there were any on the ground that is-Bloody weather!)

Chapter 31.

Chemo is not Therapy

If mastectomy surgery is the equivalent of big game hunting, cruel but quick and effective, then chemotherapy is like fighting insurgents. You take your fire power into the hillsides of Afghanistan and fire off endless blind rounds of ammunition in the hope of eradicating tiny Al Qaeda terrorists hiding out in secret caves.

Safe to say, I fear there will be considerable and prolonged collateral damage.

Chapter 32

Pet (2)

In Memory of George and Percy

Emily doesn't want a pet any more. She has exhausted all options. Gerbil? No. Tortoise? No. Komodo dragon? No. Stick insect? No. Fish? NO!!! She has simply got bored and moved on. Hypocritically, I want a pet though I really, really, really, really want a pet; specifically, I want a dog. I want a dog like I wanted a baby eleven years ago; alarm clock badly. Maybe it's a hormonal thing?

We have never had a dog in our family because Tom has pulled rank. He believes that high breed dogs need more time and care than can be achieved with full time work and school. He is absolutely right. There are, however, two solutions to this problem. Don't get a high breed dog that needs three walks a day and a pheasant shoot at the weekend, but one that is happy to lick his bollocks contentedly by the fire all day and eat biscuits. And/or I don't go to work (!) Both solutions work well for me.

I specifically want a black Labrador. I have known two black labs in my life; George and Percy. The fact that these two dogs were black labs was the beginning and the end of their similarities. George was quite simply, the loveliest, happiest, fun loving dog you could ever wish to meet. Despite, good breeding, George never showed the remotest interest in growing out of being a puppy. From a distance he could look a bit on the dumpy side until close-up you realised it was actually puppy-fat. He was a fully grown, tickle loving, black lab puppy-dog, in both appearance and character. George had two life-long hobbies; chasing Cumbrian sheep (a dangerous and life-threatening pass-time at best) and charge tackling other dogs. The former was an issue (have you ever met a Cumbrian sheep farmer), the latter was simply a curious joy to watch. This was because George, in his mind, was a canine Ma Nonu, whereas the reality was somewhat less frightening. Firstly, George couldn't actually run. This was because his back haunches never quite came to the party which meant his back side used to rotate comically, throwing him off to the side and giving him a 'two gallops forward, one swing to the side' kind of waddling running style. His speed and intent was always there, just not his technique. Secondly, he never found his inner bark. The best he could ever muster was a loud 'WOOF!' that seemed to emanate comically from his backside. His only secret weapon was his lack of ability to feel pain. This meant that despite the fact all witnesses, including the targeted dog, believed he would slow and veer away at the last minute, George had other ideas. Maybe he was the Ma Nonu of the canine world after all.

Then there was Percy; a General amongst dogs and an absolute and utter bastard towards all other dogs, which he, rightly, believed to be a shameful and embarrassing smear to his being. George got round this by playing the humble Private to Percy's General. George knew if Percy was on parade he needed to show humility, respect and a general display of his own stupidity so that Percy's condescension towards him was so great, that despite him being another male dog, he wasn't even worthy of his attention. This was actually cleverer than you might think because Percy's favourite life-long hobby was trying to kill all other male dogs. Percy had serious anger management issues and anything could flick his switch. His technique was to charge, slather and spit flying, directly at his prey and pin them by their pitiful necks against the nearest hard surface and then proceed to tear large chunks of their fur out while growling like a demented hyena. Percy was basically Jerome Kano to George's Ma Nonu.

But there was another side to Percy. Gun Dog Percy; long legged, muscled haunch, sleek black, blue furred, natural genius, Gun Dog, Percy. Tom's Dad only had to so much as flick a knee towards his gun room and Percy would leap to attention by his side, ready, superior and alert for the delicious game ahead. Percy was simply born to retrieve. Many people have said to Tom over the years what a superb gun dog Percy was, but the question of how good a dog Percy was, was not the question Percy was interested in. He didn't need telling. Percy knew. Of course he was the best gun dog you had ever seen. The question was, were you the best shot he had ever seen? In my case the answer was, no.

We used to go to a singularly unique little boat house on a lake in Coldstream, just into Scotland. It was in the middle of nowhere and you had to go through at least thirty-four gates to get to it and at least thirty four gates to go anywhere, so we didn't go anywhere; a week of solitude and contemplation, a week of langoustines, jigsaws and fly fishing.

And rabbit shooting. I know that rabbit shooting (or generally shooting any animal) is not everyone's cup of tea, but please banish images of fluffy, thumper-esque bunny rabbits from your mind. These animals were vermin. The land we shot on had more rabbits and rabbit holes than hillside – not ideal for a sheep farm. We used to have to pretend to the farmer that we had shot the two hundred, or so, daily quota which he needed to keep things under control, when actually we had done well to land a bag of no more than five or six. This is because shooting rabbits is nigh on fucking impossible. While Tom was seriously skilled, I spent most of my time raising my gun, almost pulling the trigger, and putting it back down again. I was basically out for a late evening walk with a gun. The only chance I ever had of success was if an extremely old and unusually large, ideally three-legged rabbit, decided to drag itself out of its hole for one last breath of fresh air, unable to move its aged body for at least twenty-five minutes. Then I had a tiny chance of a target. To say that Percy was unimpressed was an understatement. My lasting memory of Percy is of him standing sprung by a large heather gorse bush, inside of which he knew there was a hiding rabbit and looking condescendingly, pitifully even, up at me as if to say, "Look, lady, you and I both know I could ruck this baby out of here within the blink of an eye, but your chances of killing it are zero. Now, why don't you stop wasting my considerable skill and time on this charade, go home and leave Tom and I to the serious stuff," genuinely, no joke; all in one look.

George and Percy; R.I.P. True All blacks of their time.

Chapter 33.

In My Slipstream

I have a painting, hanging, pride of place, in my kitchen. It is a modern painting by a modern artist. It depicts two people (male? female?) I like to think female, struggling, heads bowed against the malevolent Mancunian (?) weather. Their blood red water proofs, rendered with a painterly swipe, are flipped cruelly over their heads as they struggle forward against the elements. It doesn't look like, on the face of it that they are helping each other out. They look lost in their own battles. But I know that they are. They are side by side and they have each other's backs. They are within touching distance. They are within fifty cross Pennine miles. They are within ten and a half thousand Indian Ocean miles. It doesn't matter one bit. They are in each other's slipstreams.

I love this painting, nearly as much as the person that gave it to me.

Chapter 34.

Winning the World Cup

I started out in homeland Leeds; proud to be English, with a secret crush on Mike Brown. Come on! We could do this!

Crawling embarrassingly away from group stage loss I packed my bags and nipped down to Cardiff. I cry every time at their National Anthem; I am practically from the valleys.

The boys were just too injured. So I caught a quick ferry over the Irish Sea and cracked open a Guinness. But O'Connell's men couldn't pull it off without 'our' Sexton.

So I caught a little flight to The Highlands. So, so very close. We should have, could have, won this one. Could I make it to see my sister in Sydney by Saturday? Now, over to you, my girl.

She caught a cheeky flight over to New Zealand to see friends and family for the final. Yes! We have won the World Cup!

It's exhausting being an English rugby fan.

Chapter 35.

Hockey Avoidance

In a desperate, last ditch attempt to avoid playing hockey on a Saturday for her school, Emily lied. She couldn't possibly represent her school because she went climbing with her Mum EVERY Saturday. Utter bullshit. She has NEVER been climbing with her Mum on Saturday because she can't be bothered; like she can't be bothered to play hockey. But she had made a tactical error. She appeared to have forgotten that her beloved Dad teaches at her school. This fact considerably reduces the odds of gaining success in the field of fibbing. She got caught. Dutifully scolded:-
Don't lie.
If you have to lie, don't get caught.
She went, head bowed, and still with a light huff onto the first practice, which is where she discovered, to her surprise, that there was a position in hockey that didn't involve doing any of the things she hated; namely, running anywhere and hitting a ball with a hockey stick; plus, you got to dress up like a demented polystyrene rhinoceros and intimidate everyone.
What was not to like?

To Emily's surprise, however, it turns out she loves playing goalkeeper and she is a total natural at it. She possesses the three essential skills required; quick reactions, concentration and a positive attitude (if you let a goal in, get over it quickly and move on),

So now I get to watch a hockey game every Saturday morning and I love it. I get to chat endlessly with all the other lovely Mums. I get to ogle at the male sports staff bare legs (one of them is my husband, so I can.) But best of all I get to shout out, acutely embarrassing, incorrect and untimely encouragement from the side lines (there are always subtler parenting tactics to make your child pay for wrong doing.)

GO! GO! GO! MY GOALKEEPING GIRL! GO!

GREAT SAVE MY AMAZING LITTLE ONE! MUMMY LOVES YOU!

MAN ON!

JUST WACK IT!

OFF SIDE, REF!.

I know there isn't even an off-side rule in hockey but I don't care. I love my Saturday mornings.

Chapter 36.

Advice on Lists

On the front of my current packet of Codeine Phosphate tablets there is a big red flash shouting out,

"New Advice for drivers – see leaflet inside".

I am intrigued. I wonder what the new advice is.

"Always remember to stop at red lights?"

"Don't buy a VW golf?"

The advice on the back is standard stuff;

"WARNING May cause drowsiness. If affected do not drive or operate machinery. Avoid alcoholic drink."

So, if you are an alcoholic fork-lift truck driver in pain you are basically in real trouble then. And why only heavy machinery? My hedge trimmer isn't heavy but I am not sure I should be let loose in the garden with it after taking two of these babies.

So, what's the exciting, new advice inside? I don't know because I've thrown out the leaflet. Which reminds me, I have nearly run out of my drug stash. I must write them on my list.

I love lists. I am the lady of lists. I have been known, having completed a task that I, annoyingly, had forgotten to add to my list, to add it posthumously and cross it out immediately. I am not ashamed of this. List keeping is a serious business and there are rules that must be adhered to; Never tick, ~~always cross out~~ upon completion.

Never mix your 'to buy' and your 'to do' lists. Ever. You will never witness on any list of mine, milk/eggs/washing powder/pick up dry cleaning.

No task is too mundane to make it onto a list. 'Put washing out' is a fine and worthy list item in my book.

One item does not constitute a list. This is where the trusty back up items of 'beer/wine' always come in handy.

Never be vague, especially if you are entrusting your list to others. For example, I know what 'Chopped Toms' are. In the wrong hands this will cause no end of confusion.

Chapter 37.

Results Day

I got the results from my surgery today.

I have had big results days before. Doors of varying sizes and importance opening and closing in front of me; on the whole, never turning out to be as monumental or life-changing as they seemed at the time. Probably my biggest Monsters Inc. moment was when I fell through the wrong door into Oxford University after my A level results unfortunately got me through. There was no Yeti but there were definitely some unique individuals.

There were three types of student at Oxford.

The monumentally intelligent ones who found three degree years of quantum physics a total breeze but struggled acutely with any form of human contact.

Then there were the monumentally stupid students. Those that had delivered fully on their 2 D's and 1 E un-conditional 'A' level offers. They spent term time completing the odd desperate 'all-nighter' in order to cling on to their studies and the majority of their time in taxis to London to absorb as many high class drugs as humanly possible.

Then there was me; neither monumentally brilliant nor monumentally stupid. I was the token student from 'Up North' (are you lot still down the pit up there? – genuinely asked of me during my first and only term). The state school statistic designed to keep the quota right and the Guardian off their backs.

Actually, I got into Oxford because I had impressed one of the tutors' at interview. Mrs Anne Pasternak-Slater, no less. I had somehow managed to create an artistic segue between the Canaletto Painting of Venice hanging in her office, the novel, Hotel du Lac, sitting on her desk, and the poetry of Alexander Pope; the subject of my entrance essay. I have no memory of how, or why, I did this, but it gave her the (incorrect) but desired impression that I was hugely and diversely well read. Mrs APS turned out to be an extremely scary lady. She came from the Mrs Robinson school of tutoring; she oozed sexuality, and not in a good way. In one tutorial she called an abrupt and premature end to the session, declaring us all to be, "Far too intense and repressed." and demanded that we should all "get out her office immediately and go and find someone to fuck!" Er, ok.

Mrs Robinson was not the only unique and intimidating tutor I encountered during my brief stay. I was 'taught' (I use this the term lightly) Victorian Literature by a lady whose name escapes me but who was apparently a leading light on Thomas Hardy. How she achieved this was a mystery to me because I never saw her move from her reclining position on her 'chase longue' the entire term. She reminded me of a tiny bird that had fallen from its nest; its skeletal little bones left spread-eagled at strange angles where it had fallen. It's huge, puffy, pink, boiled egg eyes, squinting sorrowfully out at the cruel world. This sorry state meant that she was obviously unable to take, read, mark or comment on any of our essays. The tutorial used to consist of us knocking very quietly on the door, tip-toeing in as silently as we could, and reading our essays out-loud to her, and then leaving. The painfulness of this experience was only exacerbated by the fact that we had all been paired with another student. My partner was Hugo R Francis. Hugo attended all tutorials in a dark purple, silk, smoking jacket and I never understood even one word of his extensive essays. This was because Hugo was obsessed with the Metaphysical Poets and Franz Kafka and was determined to interweave both passions into the works of George Elliot whether 'bird lady' liked it or not.

My Old English tutor was no less unique. Blessed with the brilliant name, Vincent Gillespie, I never actually saw his face directly as it was permanently shrouded in a cloud of peach flavoured tobacco from the pipe that never left his mouth the entire time. Old English had its charms but it was just too tempting to cheat given the fact that the aim of the game was to pass the end of term exam which was to translate sections of Beowulf into English. The place was heaving in contraband exam papers which you could pick up for a fiver and learn off by heart and attain your 'A' without having to have even a passing understanding of any actual Old English.

No less unique than my tutors were my house mates. Living below me was a chap named McCormack

McCormack. McCormack's favourite pastime was to regale to me how he had a serious and life threatening addiction to Newcastle Brown Ale. An incongruous problem, I remember thinking, for a Scotsman.

Above me were our two lesbian lovers. Their favourite pastime was to bathe together and shave each other's legs (and I suspected other things.) The output of which evidenced itself as a thick hairy, immovable black line round the only bath in the house. Lovely.

To my left was Eton Olly. Olly looked like a small injured panda. The bags round his eyes he got, I suspect, from reading the Financial Times all day and all night and worrying endlessly, to anyone who cared to listen, which FTSE 100 company he would work for when he graduated.

And finally, finishing off the ring of weirdness was the neighbour to my right, Marcus. Marcus despised his father but put up with him because he kept him in supplies of the only filter less French cigarettes he condescended to smoke. Marcus's favourite pastime was to creep into my room when I dared to go to the loo and leave scented notes on my desk. "You and I, how about it? Fancy getting warm tonight? Etc, etc, etc. Safe to say I never got to know Marcus. As soon as I was able, that Xmas, I sledged, Mike Wazowski styl-ee right out of there!

And so to today's important results. It turns out that I actually had four mini-tumours masquerading on my mammogram as one big Mama Tumour. My auxiliary node and two of his buddies had also done a heroic job of being brave bouncers and denied any further access. (Remaining four nodes all clear.) Because I am young and there is still no guarantee that an errant cancer cell has not slipped un-noticed under the door to start its own party I am still to have chemo.

I am fine with this. I have two weeks to get fit before I start eighteen weeks of six rounds. Let's go.

Chapter 38.

Academic Hopes and Isotopes

In my middle class drop out months, between Oxford and York University, I worked at a bookshop in Manchester. My personal view was that this bookshop was no more than a thin veil covering up the true, shadier business at hand. The owner had obviously been sent undercover by his Government to steal Manchester University's leading research into Isotope Geochemistry. We only ever got paid out of the till and we carried out a full stock take every other week. All the signs were there.

Working in this bookshop had its moments. One of the highlights was watching the pale-faced first year Law Students break out into a warm sweat upon realising that their fifty-two long compulsory first term reading list consisted entirely of hard back books over nine hundred and twenty pages long. It was great fun watching them fervently ring their Daddies to help them carry them all out of the shop.

Customer service, however, had its challenges. Remember, this was an academic book shop. Your average customer was not popping in to pick up the latest edition of 'Fifty Shades of Gray.' The required book was always written on a small piece of paper,

"Oh hi, have you got this in stock, please? Neodymium Isotope Geochemistry: Isotopes as Tracers in Planetary Evolution." You knew even before reading the title the answer was, "No." We never had anything in stock that anybody actually wanted but it was important to pretend.

The first step was to take the customer to the section that most likely corresponded to the title. Gardening? Botany? Geology? Chemistry? I didn't have a bloody clue. You then had to pretend that you believed you would find said title and were only moments away from plucking it victoriously from the shelves – two or three minutes was always enough to convince. "No, I am afraid it doesn't look like we have this one in stock, sorry. We could order it for you?" The customer would then, innocently, enquire, "How long will it take to come in do you think?" and I would reply, "Honestly? Never. It will never come in if you actually want this book. No matter how many times you ring us to check. If, however, you don't really want this book and you have no intention of coming back in to pick it up, I guarantee it will arrive tomorrow and join the other twenty thousand books stashed below this desk." We had more books waiting for collection than we had on the shelves.

This is probably why the bookshop sadly no longer exists. Mind you, neither does Manchester University's leading position on Isotope Geochemistry. Who knew?

Chapter 39.

Cancer makes you fat

Not because of the drugs or the forced sedentary lifestyle; but because of the cake, lovely, out-sized, unctuous sugary cake that loved ones' bake and send to you. A card is not hard; a cake is baked with you in mind, all the while you are beating and whisking and mixing and waiting and willing for the rise you are thinking and caring about me. Thank you.

Ginger cake the size of a hockey pitch, left like Moses at midday by my front door waiting to be loved.

More ginger cake; bold and beautiful arriving by post wrapped in bubble wrap and flat packed pampers boxes to protect its sweetness. Ripped off like bread in ragged chunks and wrapped in foil to be consumed with fireworks and sloe gin in the dark.

The best chocolate cake known to man smuggled over The Pennines on a wet and windy day and eaten by cheeky eighths with afternoon tea.

Fruitcake snug in its old Cadbury roses Xmas box. Wet and sticky with fruit, abstained on until evening and a glass of wine. All mine.

Chapter 40.

I am an Expert in my Field, let me tell you

I know a great deal about procurement. I am a member of the Chartered Institute of Procurement and Supply (MCIPS). I graduated with a distinction, no less. Are you interested? I very much doubt it. This is the thing about specialism. It is monumentally interesting and relevant to those inside and quite spectacularly coma-inducing boring to those on the outside. I know this, which is why, I very rarely find myself trying to take up anyone's time on the finer points of supply management. But what amazes me is there are many individuals who don't seem to realise that their area of passion is strangely of no interest whatsoever to others. Enter our new boiler fitter.

A lovely man; warm, friendly, professional, and an utter, arm eating bore when it came to the extensive subject of choosing and fitting a boiler. I am ashamed to admit that I abdicated total responsibility to Tom on this one. Two hours into the lecture on the finer details of Valliant V Smart weather compensating control systems and Tom had lost the will to live. It was cruel but impossible to resist to keep popping in to ask innocent questions just to prolong the torture; "Please, tell me more, do, about the Eco Tec 28kw boiler 7 year guarantee, it is so, so interesting."

I have come across specialist bores before. The best was the chap who came to sell us our double glazed kitchen 'barn' door. This gentleman was wearing, with zero irony, a tie with pictures of PCs on it. We should have read the warning signs. He loved doors in a way that was not normal. When we had finally selected our model – he flushed up with joy and ran out to his car, returning with a nifty over the shoulder bag. He took a deep breath and unzipped the thing slowly - the suspense was high – "This, ladies and gentleman, is just a sample." and it was; just a sample of the bloody door. We didn't care anymore. We just wanted our lives back. We bought the bloody door – it cost a lot. It was a beautiful door. It did everything a door could possibly do; which is the problem, I suppose. It opened. It closed. The top half opened while the bottom half closed (barn door mode) and it locked. And it unlocked. Brilliant.

Boilers boil water and let water un-boil.

I procure things (or used to) which is only a posh word for buying things.

Doors fill gaps in walls so you can get in and out. End of story.

Chapter 41.

You do bottom up, I'll do top down

Happy and fulfilling long term relationships are about compromise; give and take, helping each other out, understanding each other's needs.

Tom plays five-a-side football on a Monday night. Contrary to what people may think; that this game is a step down from the proper, youthful, full pitch, eleven-a-side game, five-a-side football is hard core. There might be a few more beer bellies knocking about and possibly a few more that fake injury induced substitutions but the ball never goes out of play. I mean never. The game never stops. Is there another sport where this is the case? I can't think of one. There are no throw-ins, line-outs, kicks into touch, serves - nothing to induce a rest - for many, many minutes. The ref; there is actually a ref, has absolutely nothing to do. Most of the time he appears to hang around the half way line having a fag. Secondly, you get 'stuck in'. I mean, properly stuck in. This is not netball.

Usually, the after effects of Monday night for Tom are no more than a seven-hour unstoppable sweat, but last night he got tackled by an eighteen stone mid-fielder whose understanding of the more technical elements of the game seemed a bit light - which is more than can be said of the impact of his knee meeting Tom's leg.

By eight o'clock Tom had a large log for a right leg. Sat in his boxers with a pack of peas on his knee he was feeling sorry for himself. Er, where has my post op 24/7 care got to? Role reversal time; except, problem; I am only working properly from the middle down.

But we made it through the night. Tom covered off everything that required upper body movement and/or strength and I covered off everything that involved travel and/or bending.

If the postman had only rung (twice?) this morning, he would have had the unique vision of seeing me trying to put Tom's socks on for him while he simultaneously worked me successfully out of my pyjamas top.

Jack Nicholson and Jessica Lang we are not.

Chapter 42.

Two by Two

My body is a bit beaten up but my soul is soaring. I put it down to walking. The thing about walking is it slows things down; your nose is close to the ground (quite close in my case being a short arse), you get to see things, smell things, hear things that you would normally whizz past and consider too mundane for observation.

I like sniffing out the secret snickets that lie quietly hidden, hatched across the bolder, busier roads. They appear like faded forgotten scars; reminders of an ancient, more on-foot time. They smuggle you under motorways, not giving two hoots about the rush hour traffic and shove you out the other side into wide open green fields. Brilliant.

Over the last week of walks this is what I have seen:-

Two pairs of jays (flashes of brilliant, underwing blue).

Two woodpeckers (flying not pecking).

Two herons (lazy ragged wings blackening the sky).

Two hares (different fields same nonchalance).

Two monumental bulls (not in the same field, obviously).

Two robin redbreasts (my favourite).

Two wild teal (flying in for tea).

Two irritable scruffy farm dogs (given a very wide berth).

And guess what the landlord at the Star Inn where I just HAD to pop in to sup 2 x cheeky halves of Farmers Blonde while doing the X 2 cryptic crossword was called?

……………………………………..NOAH!

Naaaaaaaa! He wasn't really, he was called Dave.

Oh, well.

Chapter 43.

Graphs, Columns and Lady Luck

I saw my Oncologist yesterday; a lovely, funny, positive lady. She checked over my scar. In the limited and not very attractive world of mastectomy scars mine was proclaimed as rather beautiful. What am I going to do with all these compliments over my appearance?

She drew me two columns on a piece of paper; one headed up with a G for good and one headed up with a B for bad. I had considerably more in the good column than the bad. Hoorah! It made me feel good – I am sure this was the aim. Surgery successful = good. No longer have cancer = good. HER2 negative = good. PR7 and ER8 positive = good. Young and fit = good. Apart from the Bloody, Buggery, Badness of having cancer in the first place (this was left out of the B column) the only not so good fact was that it had travelled to x 3 of my lymph nodes. But she even found a positive in this fact as apparently the surgeon managed to remove all the nodes at 'level 3' (highest level away from breast, apparently) and all these were clear. I love this lady.

And then she showed me the dreaded prognosis graphs. Or the 'how long have you got to live, do we think', graphs; five years looks relatively rosy. Out of one hundred women who have what I have/had 75% survive just with surgery. Happy days. With chemo and hormone therapy the line gets even longer. Ten years; not so pretty. It's 50/50 with only surgery. I don't like 50/50 it sounds more like a punt than odds. With chemo this gets shunted up to 64% and with hormone therapy a much more reassuring 76%. 50% is a Desmond 3rd. 64% is an average 2:1 but 76% is a shiny 1st class honours so the decision was easy; bring on the therapies.

Plus, I've been thinking. Bad ass stats are fine but at the end of the day that is all they are. They don't frighten me because they don't know everything. Most of us can only really squint into our futures with a mixture of faith and philosophy and a bloody tight grip of Lady Luck's hand. So that is what I am doing.

Chapter 44.

His and Hers Hematomas

When Tom and I got married, Tom's brother, Ben, made a very funny and very true best man speech. The overriding theme was the bride and groom's innate competitiveness with each other. "They are probably even competing at getting married, right now!" was the line that got the most laughs. Ha! Ha! It wasn't true. We weren't competing; not at getting married anyway. We were, on that particular day, competing at sweating.

Tom and I got married on a humid, hot August Day. One of those days when the sky is white not blue and the sun doesn't shine so much as sear. What little fresh air there was didn't make it into the lovely little chapel we got married in. I had chosen a dress that was, to put it mildly; simple. So simple that underwear would not have remained a secret. So I wasn't wearing any. It also had no back. While kneeling in front of the vicar, during our vows I was sweating hard trying to stop the sweat making its way, in full view of the congregation, down my bare back and beyond.

Tom, on the other hand, was sweating (and shaking) because he had been up until 4.30 in the morning, drinking and impersonating Elvis.

Tom won.

And so, thirteen years later, here we are, still competing. How funny. How tragic. I have a stubborn hematoma under my arm that despite drains and secondary surgery has clenched its fist hard and is refusing to soften. Joy. The sensation can only be described as like having your under-arm gradually tightened in a vice. You know those things that you used to use in woodwork lessons at school? I hated woodwork. I always started out with such grand plans. I would make a wooden car; life size. Problem being; the only woodwork skill I had was planing. Three weeks in my plans had moderated. I would make a toy car; two more weeks of planing. No, I would make a toy car for one of my little sister's toys; a toy's toy car. As the end of term approached I had a tiny weenie microscopic wooden car, thingy. And then finally the inevitable stage; I had nothing – an invisible wooden car. Every time; planing a hematoma is not an option. But hitting it with drugs and rest is. Two days after getting it checked out I am already feeling a million times better.

And so to my lovely husbands competing hematoma; how anyone can make footy knee to knee contact result in such bruising is a mystery to me. Empathy is one thing, but this is ridiculous. As I heal nicely, Tom has an ankle to thigh discolouring that knocks my trauma into touch.

Bloody hell. He beats me at everything.

Chapter 45.

Cap or Cloche?

I have been hat hunting today; in preparation for temporary baldness. I don't like hats. Or rather hats don't like me much. I don't know whether it is the arch of my brow or that my ears are too small/too high on my head. I am just not one of those people who can nonchalantly throw on a hat at a jaunty angle and look faintly fabulous and/or endearingly eccentric. It's just not me. Maybe it's because you have to believe, and deep down I am not totally convinced by all things hat. While there are those that believe them to be accessories I secretly believe hats to be excessive; hinting at a little too much face time in the mirror. I have never, ever observed someone in an outfit and thought to myself, 'what that look is crying out for to hit perfection is a hat;' ever. You only have to go to a wedding to question the sanity of it all. Seemingly the more money spent; the bigger and more silly the hat gets. And then there are fascinators. Don't get me started. Has there ever been anything less aptly named than a fascinator? Princess Beatrice. Royal Wedding. Enough said.

'Chemo hats' are a separate area of no-go fashion. Choices are three fold.

One; the head scarf; these range from the 'Yasser Arafat' through to the 'Audrey Hepburn' via the 'Maggie Thatcher'. Not tempted.

Second choice is the turban; seemingly, with or without a frontal brooch. If someone is not a hat lover it goes without saying that the world of brooches will not have been broached.

To put the two together brings me out in a slight sweat.

The final choice is the cloche. What a brilliant, but faintly rude sounding word; French for bell, apparently; back in fashion thanks to Downton Abbey, along with corsets and cravats. No thank you.

While I clearly have a problem with fashion and chemo hats; essential hats are fine with me.

> Hard hats for walking under hard heavy things - fine.
>
> Woolly winter hats to keep warm - fine.
>
> Swimming hats for streamlining - fine.
>
> Sun hats for shade - fine.
>
> Baseball caps for baseball etc - fine. All fine.

But it's not all fine, really because I have a secret. I may be suspicious of hats when it comes to buying and wearing but I have to admit I am a secret hat-tryer-on-er. I LOVE trying hats on; the more unsuitable and terrible the better. Call me a hat hating hypocrite, I don't care. I normally have my daughter right behind me to keep me in check with a curt, "Mum, take it off, you are SO embarrassing." But not today; today I can really let rip. Below is a list of all the hats I tried on today (and didn't buy, obviously).

> A strange top hat that made me look like a cross between Abraham Lincoln and Johnny Depp (in or not in Alice in Wonderland.)

A lovely leopard hat resplendent with long army things doubling up as gloves (I was tempted by this.)
A heavy peaked black baseball hat that made me look like one of Justine Bieber's fake friends.
A Peaky Blinder flat cap (just needed the waistcoat and fag to complete.)
A strange flat red hat that made me look like the Duke of Urbino in Piero della Francesca's famous portrait.
A brilliant purple bucket hat that made me look like LL Cool J (minus the Mercedes jewellery and bad Kappa tracksuit.)
A strange little black bowler hat (I have a problem with these hats as I immediately turn into Oddjob and try to assassinate shop keepers.)
A strange floppy, stripey woolly hat that made me look like Dr Suess's iconic cat. (I was tempted by this one, too.)

Below is a list of the hats I actually bought:
Boring woolly bobble hat - black (to go with the five I already had).
Boring woolly bobble hat - cream (to go with the six I already had).
Boring woolly bobble hat - grey (to go with the seven I already had).

After chemotherapy, radiotherapy and hormone therapy, I wonder whether there is such thing as hat therapy.

Chapter 46.

Can I introduce you to my Good Friend, Larry Listerine?

The lovely lady that served me today in Lloyds Pharmacy had probably the worst case of halitosis I have ever had the misfortune to come into close contact with.

I suspect if you were to carry out a survey of one hundred Yorkshire men and women and ask them the question; have you, or have you ever had, bad breath, it would return a big fat confident zero. If, however, you were to ask the question, do you know, or have you ever known, anyone with stinky breath, it would be in the high 90's. While our noses are sound centurions at picking up all smells both good and bad emanating from other people and things when it comes to our own breath, our noses just are not up to it. This is a problem, because one thing is for sure absolutely no-one is going to tell us.

When my lovely lady asked me whether there was anything else she could do for me I honestly nearly passed out, "No thank y-" was all I could manage as I staggered backwards and wrenched my scarf un-subtly over my nose. The world is full of poor unfortunate halitosis suffers who wonder, in quiet moments, why their social life has never been as vibrant as they would have liked. Why they have never quite made it to the top of their career ladders. Mr Saunders, twenty-five years a teacher, has always wondered why his popularity with the kids has never scaled the heights of his colleagues. Little does he know he has been called 'Stinky-sprout-breath-Saunders' for the past two decades. Cruel but true.

What I actually should have done upon being orally napalmed by my pharmacist is tell the truth and send her into a better life. Stepping bravely forward, gripping the counter for confidence and leaning into the death zone, I should have replied, "Well, now that you mention it, there is something you can do for me, yes. For starters, take this packet of Mentos that you, oh so, ironically are selling across your counter and eat them. In fact, here, eat three packets. Then, go home tonight and check over your diet because something just isn't working. Finally, to cover all bases, get yourself an appointment with your dentist." How rude. Can you just imagine her reaction if I had said this? Just like halitosis's sisters, body odour and low hanging bogeys, there is absolutely no way anyone will ever tell you the truth. Not ever. This is because we are British. We have invented a whole lexicon of euphemisms, to avoid mutual blushes for even the most innocuous social faux pas.

Take the scenario of spotting a colleague with his, or her, flies down; a fairly low level, temporary, sartorial faux pas. Do we say, "Mate, your zips undone; sort it out." No, far too rude. We say, "Mate, you're flying low", or "You've got egg on your face" Or my absolute favourite, "You've got windows in your laptop." The problem with bad breath is it's strangely euphemism free. If well-established euphemisms existed, I could have saved my pharmacist. I could have let her know the truth kindly and subtly; "I hope you don't mind me pointing this out, but I believe you may need to train your dragon." Or, "It appears your Aquafresh has gone AWOL." Or, "Can I introduce you to my good friend Larry Listerine?" It would have spared my lovely pharmacist undue embarrassment. Upon hearing these words, she would have been able to smile sweetly and thank me for letting her know. I would have been able to nod conspiratorially and leave quietly; my good deed for the day done. Instead, I am ashamed to admit, all I did was add mints and mouth wash to my list of purchases in the vain attempt that she would take the hint.

Chapter 47.

Aldi-isms

Three things happen, without exception, to everyone who shops at Aldi for the first time. Firstly, everyone thinks they are the first customers to have discovered Aldi; ever. "Everything is so cheap!" they cry. "There are no brands! Did you know there are no brands?" "I even bought some frozen clams, can you believe it. Frozen clams!" They turn into the Captain Scott of supermarket shopping.

The second thing that happens is they purchase a selection of goods that wouldn't look out of place on Larry Grayson's Generation Game.

A cuddly toy-Check.

An over-sized cabbage-Check.

A blow up beach-ball-Check.

Bird seed-Check.

The final thing that happens is that they have to subject their family to an endless game of The Price is Right. And I mean endless.

All three of these things happened to Tom last week upon his first visit to the wondrous world of Aldi. Sitting quietly and contently reading the paper in the lounge I was subjected to Tom bouncing into the doorway proudly holding up a jar of red cabbage. "How much? Guess! Go on!" Oh, I don't know, "£7.20?" "No!!! 98p! Can you believe it?" and off he bounced. Two minutes of peace and he was back again holding proud and high a bottle of washing up liquid. "Go on! Have a guess!" I decided to play along, "64p?" "Nope! 50p!" Back he bounded a third time with a can of furniture polish, "28p. 28p! How amazing is that?" And so on; a bottle of Chateauneuf-du-Pape. A chilled quiche Lorraine. Japanese cabbage. Chocolate Mousse. How long was this going to last? He was like Tigger with discount tourettes. Eventually I had to subtly hint that while I was indeed impressed with both the price and range of his purchases I didn't want to guess the price of every single one of them really.

The thing is, I know quite a lot about supermarkets having worked on the inside of one for eleven years. I know all their evil tricks. So I am not fooled by Aldi; poor, simple, lovely Aldi, working so hard to give us value goods. They can't even afford shelving or staff. Putting two fingers up to the big nasty brands and listing lovely small tertiary products. Aaaahh. Don't be fooled. Their motivation is the same; expansion, global domination and profit, like all other multi-national businesses. Aldi made £260m profit last year. It's no warm hearted SME let me tell you. It might not be as scary as Tesco (yet) but the wolf is the same just dressed in lambs clothing, or probably in the case of Aldi an amazingly priced polyester jumper for a quid.

Chapter 48.

Wig Watching

It serves me right, really. If you have spent any of your formative years reading Viz and laughing cruelly at the jokes that you know would offend your Mother, then you probably deserve your come-up-ance at some point in your life.

I had mine last Tuesday. Is she or is she not wearing a wig? Yes she is; and a lovely stocking over her head to keep her real hair down as it hasn't fallen out yet. One of the perks of cancer treatment on the NHS is you get your very own free wig. And not any wig, a Raquel Welch designer wig, no less. Did you know the lovely Raquel Welch designed wigs? Did you know she was even still alive?

When I was called into my very own Wig Corner, the room was covered with a smorgasbord of synthetic creations. I have never seen as many hair pieces in my entire life. The mind boggled as to how some of these creations could possibly ever pass as hair but there we go. Not particularly wanting to channel the aging Hollywood hanger-on look, my choice of false bonce covers was rather limited; to two to be precise. One that made me look a bit like 'The Hoff' and the one I chose which I thought looked bloody great; if you didn't know me, the lights were dim, you were fairly short sighted and not very observant.

Having made my choice of one from one, I was given a short seminar on the fine art of placing your wig on your head. This may sound a simple task but it is riddled with risk. Strangely, if you place it perfectly on your bonce it looks fine, however, if you get it just even one inch skewiff you immediately look like Phil Spector. Not a look I was after. My lovely wig fitting lady was clearly over the moon with my choice (?) She even suggested I could accessorise it with an Alice band. Bless. It crossed my mind to ask her whether her range extended to Merkins just to see the look on her face, but I changed my mind at the last minute.

I will probably keep my wig appearances limited to the odd shopping trip rather than confuse my friends and family. I have tried it on for Tom who is far from convinced. To my horror he shared a picture of Michael Fabricant with me and the similarity is disconcerting to say the least. I have also tried it on Emily's favourite teddy who bizarrely looks very natural. For now, it is nestled, like a warm, hibernating squirrel in my bedside draw, happy to make an appearance if required.

Chapter 49.

Echo Nurse

I had my first round of chemotherapy yesterday. Administered over an hour and half by a fantastic, Yorkshire and riotously blunt nurse called Michelle. I loved her from the moment she opened her mouth and introduced herself, “Hi, Lucy, I’m Michelle, how are you? Are you well? Well, obviously you’re not well are you or you wouldn’t be here!” Fantastic; Yorkshire through and through. Love it.

Michelle’s first, usually straightforward task was to locate a suitably juicy and willing vein in my left hand. Not as straightforward as you would imagine. Apparently when hands are cold the veins avoid the surface, a bit like fishing for river trout on a cold winter’s day, then? Answer? Bring in the hand warmer. Now I know the NHS is a bit strapped for cash but this contraption looked like something Sir Alan Sugar would have been proud to patent in the 80’s. It consisted of a blue plastic blanket-ee thing attached by a thick black wire to a black box that basically looked like a detonator with big red numbers dictating the temperature. I was well prepared for the calculated dangers of chemo but not the chances of getting blown up by a short circuiting hand warmer!

Someone else who had clearly never seen a hand warmer before was my lovely supporting nurse; let’s affectionately call her Echo Nurse. Firstly, she tried to fit my hand inside the warmer and then promptly gave up. Had she never seen a blanket before? It really wasn't that complex. It was her first day on the ward. We know this because she told everyone; many times. To say she was a little on the under-confident side is an under-statement. Her only apparent skill was to repeat timidly every single question Michelle asked me immediately after Michelle had just asked me. Michelle: "Are you allergic to anything, Lucy?" Me: "No." Cue Echo Nurse:" Are you allergic to anything, Lucy?" Me: "Er, no." Tom got a disloyal smirk out of Michelle when he pointed out that if I had become allergic to something in the five seconds between the first time I was asked and the second it was the fastest onset of any allergic reaction ever.

Now that my hand was warm and toasty in a way that was clearly more conventional, and a lot safer, methods such as hot water and/or gloves could not have delivered, it was time to hunt out my veins again. But still, this was beyond Michelle. Subtle as ever she hollered for the ward sister, "I need you to come and dig out Lucy's veins for her!" DIG!? Gulp. Enter, 'The Ward Sister'. Filling every stereotype in every stride as she confidently made her way towards me she sat down (her knees had most definitely never ever met each other) squarely in front of me, took one disapproving look at my wimpy, veinless hand and got to work. I looked away, but 10 painless seconds later we were in and ready to flow; thank you sister.

Before we could get going I had to be checked for the millionth time to ensure I was who they thought I was. Michelle: "Name and date of birth, please, Lucy." Me: "lucyverinder25thofthe8th73." Wait for it...................... Echo Nurse: "Name and date of birth please, Lucy." Tom! Don't you dare!

A pleasant hour and half of endless warm, funny and blunt banter with Michelle and it was over. The highlight being when Michelle warned me that I might feel 'A tingling feeling down below!' during the first stage. "Tell me if you do, love, apparently it's quite pleasant!" Er, okay. Starting with a litre bag of saline to dilute the nasty stuff and trick my body into thinking it was just here for a spot of hydration. Then moving on to a bout of steroids and anti-sickness drugs and then finishing with six and a half novelty sized syringes full of disturbingly Aztec red liquid, diluted down via a second tube with water and salt. And when it had finished? Of course Michelle asked me, "Well? Did you feel anything down below, then?"

I was finally packed off with a party bag of take-home drugs and an invitation to my next session; Christmas Eve, no less. It's an exclusive invite list; only bald, pale, ill guest allowed. I might bring some crackers and minced pies. Maybe a few pressies as well; a copy of 'Echo Beach' by Martha and the Muffins for Echo Nurse and the 'Art of Being Subtle' by Sharlyn Lauby for Michelle. I am quite looking forward to it actually.

Chapter 50.

Desmond doesn't do it for me

I don't like windy weather at all. At best it irritates me. At worst it worries me. Last night's gales created a cacophony of noises until the early hours; the errant television aerial wire thrashing itself incessantly against the side of the house. Two tiles shuffling frustratingly on the corner of the roof. The conservatory roof whipped up to let in the wind whistling like a children's zip wire; and finally the two colossal conifers in next door's gardens mockingly waving at us. Could they withstand the gales? So we do what everyone does when it sounds a lot worse than it is; batten down the hatches, draw the curtain tight, light the fire and put the TV on louder than normal and thank our lucky stars we don't live in Cockermouth or Carlisle. Again.

Oh, and we do one more thing. We give the storm a stupid and utterly incongruous name. Like Desmond. Maybe we give storms such pathetic names to make us feel less scared by them. In the same way as we want to rename ISIS so that it reminds us less of our Halifax savings accounts, giving a storm a silly name convinces us it might not be the beginning of some really Biblical weather that reminds us we are really small and weak. I mean how much damage can a Desmond do for goodness sake? Look at Desmond's through history; Tu-tu, O'Conner, Lynam. Nice chaps but they don't exactly put the fear of God into you do they? I imagine a tired old chap in a grey suit and specs sat in the Met Office thumbing through a huge worn-out book of Storm Names charged with having to pick the most un-prepossessing title for the next storm making its way from the Mexican Gulf.

Actually I have looked into this and the reality is no less silly. In 1953 the US abandoned a confusing plan to name storms by a phonetic alphabet when a new international phonetic alphabet was introduced and just started using any female names for storms. The practice of naming storms only after women came to an end in 1978 when men's names were included in the Eastern North Pacific Storm list and then in 1979 male and female names were included in lists for the Atlantic and Gulf of Mexico; fascinating.

Even more fascinating, there is a strict procedure for naming Tropical Storms set out by an international committee (no less) of the World Meteorological Organisation. Six lists are used in rotation and re-cycled every six years, i.e., the 2014 list will be used again in 2020. The only time that there is a change in the list is if a storm is so deadly or costly that the future use of its name on a different storm would be inappropriate for reasons of sensitivity. If that occurs, then at an annual meeting by the WMO committee the offending name is stricken from the list and another name is selected to replace it. Brilliantly, several names have been retired since the lists were created and a good thing too, just look at some of these names;

Bob – retired 1991

Dennis – retired 2005
Keith – retired 2000
Lenny – retired 1999
Roxanne – retired 1995
Wilma – retired 2005

Come on! I could do better than that. If I was on the WMO committee, I would introduce a few much more interesting selection methods. First system; name storms after Rugby League Players. Steele Retchless (London Broncos 1998-2004.) Now there's a name for a storm. If you heard that this baby was making its way from the Pacific Basin to your garden, you would sit up and notice wouldn't you? It beats 'Bob' any way. "Junior Paramore is threatening to batter the North West Coast of the British Isles this evening. Not as big as his father, Senior Paramore but still able to wreak serious damage." Again, you would get your sandbags at the ready wouldn't you?

System number two; name storms with the same methodology used to create your Porn Star Name. Everyone knows this game; take your first pets name and then your maiden name; works its magic every time. We did this years ago with a great group of friends and came up with some beauties'

Flipper Target
Pinky Wall
Lottie Grieves
Tuck Rudge
Tia Maria McFarlen

You would never need to retire these names.

"Pinky Wall is squalling aggressively out in the Atlantic. We are now on an amber warning!"

"Flipper Target has our shores in its sights as it threatens to hit the North East Coast of England!"

When I am through with this Chemo business I am going to write to the WMO for a job. They clearly need me.

Chapter 51.

Tortellini Ears

I have never given much consideration to my ears. Other than to muse on their lack of assistance towards my hat wearing ability, that is. They are quite unremarkable, really; not too big, not too small, not too sticky-outy. They have certainly never given me any real cause for concern. That is until I lost my hair and at the same time gained an inconvenient half inch of space behind each of my ears. This phenomenon has the curious effect of making my ears fold over excruciatingly painfully when I lie down and go to sleep. No matter how many times I smooth them neatly out, when I wake up they are both scrunched up into two neat tortellini ear shapes. It is quite bizarre. The pain is not short term, either. It is similar in length to waking up having slept on your arm and given yourself full bore pins and needles. While the blood ambles slowly back and your body gradually remembers how it should be functioning, the pain is truly unique. Who knew the real reason we need hair on our heads.

Another unwanted side effect to all this is reflux. I am not talking a little lukewarm reverse air - pop a quick Gaviscon - and you're good to go - reflux, here. This is major gas works. My gut has turned satanic and is hell bent on converting even the smallest morsel of food into caustic acid and trying to hurl it back up at me. Worse, it is cruelly playing with me. Sometimes, it tricks me into a false sense of security that it will do its job placidly and efficiently - it was only a rhubarb yoghurt for crying out loud- and I am back on the digestive wagon, but then at the last minute it will decide it can't be bothered and whip up a bowling ball sized of gas that nearly knocks me sideways. I think it's the hope that hurts the most.

The final unwritten side effect that I am really enjoying at the moment, which I fear may be more long term, are my ribs. Having unintentionally lost well over ten lbs in weight, only a few of which I probably needed to shed, I can see my ribs. I am not talking about the little pretty parallel ones that curve sensibly across my torso under my arm; the ones that tragically some women strive to reveal. I mean the serious, jaggedy iggledy-piggedly ones that curve round into your sternum. These, not so attractive ribs, should be nicely hidden under breast fat and muscle. Not mine, I am afraid. Peculiarly, I look a bit like half a sacred Hindu cow.

On the positive side, however, I haven't had an alcoholic drink for four months. I am on the diet of a Trappist Monk minus the mead. I am getting at least thirteen hours kip a night and my eyes haven't set sight on a frustrating spreadsheet or annoying work email for months. If it wasn't for the fact that I am poisoning myself with rounds of toxins, I am healthier than I have ever been.

Chapter 52

The She Boiler gets it

Today was an especially lovely day. One of the only advantages of feeling so poorly is that when you don't anymore, every little thing takes on a delicious treacly edge.

First joyous event of the day was watching my boiler man rip the She Boiler out. I swear I heard her drag her long nails down the wall as she desperately tried to hang on to her perch. It's over, lady. I hope she could just see out, from where she was trashed in the back of the van to witness the arrival of the new He Boiler. Not a dial in site. Fully remote controlled via iPhone app, no less; docile, obedient and definitely all male.

Second fun activity of the day; shopping for stocking fillers. As Emily hangs on greedily to the good sides of Father Christmas Faith, stockings still need to be filled. Every year I try so hard to be original but every year I get the irresistible traditional pull of tangerine and Terry's Chocolate Orange. It is futile to resist. Town had that strange suspended atmosphere that takes over one week from Christmas. As if everyone and everything is holding its breath ahead of the inevitable retail Armageddon. I indulged where necessary with Sainsbury's lovely ranges of golden leafed minced pies, Christmas Puds and various indulgent and obviously totally un-needed goodies.

And then I did something I haven't done in forty-two years. I went to the Cinema on my own. Like most Mum's, the majority of films I have seen in the last 10 years have been animated and funny but over the last four months I am veraciously filling in my decade long gap of film watching, and loving it. I had always considered, whenever, infrequently, I had considered it that going to the cinema solo was quite sad. But when you think about it is not really a social pastime. Anyway, I and three other solo cinema goers had a hilarious two hours watching Sisters. Very rarely have I watched a film that is laugh out loud as frequently as this film. There is a doomed comedy sex scene involving an inflammable Chinese lucky fortune cat and a ballerina music box that had me nearly choking on my hot dog.

To continue the theme of going solo, I then went for half a Guinness at the Kings Arms on the Heath. Again, a pastime possibly considered strange for a lone female; but today appeared to be a day of solo firsts. I was even propositioned at the bar by two 70+ year olds who had clearly been drinking snugly in their snug bar for more than a few hours. "You look cold, there, love. Come in here and we will warm you up!" "Lovely thought but, er, no thanks." I smiled sweetly and politely turned them down. I took my half pint of black gold and settled by the fire in the main bar. The King's Arms' pub is an extremely lovely but very, very dark pub. It is ineffectively lit only by gas light. So on a dark day outside it is a dark day inside. Too dark to read the paper which is what I wanted to do. The brightest thing in the room, by a country mile and more, was the Xmas tree. I have never in all my life seen such a manically lit Xmas tree. This thing would not have looked out of place on stage with the Chemical Brothers. Its migraine inducing flashing was laughingly incongruous in a pub lit only by gas light. On the plus side it created more than enough blue and white laser light to read the paper by.

I was back home just in time to settle down to a forty-minute lecture on how to control the new He Boiler via my phone. I was trying to give him my best Chemo pain face to speed him up but boiler man was impervious to my shameful tricks. Safe to say I can now plan my 'daily heating schedule' while in the cinema or in the pub. Amazing.

The remainder of the week is an extremely sociable one.

Chapter 53.

Watery Tales

Tom and Emily go swimming up at their school every Sunday; one of the many advantages of teaching at a private school with lovely facilities, a private swimming pool of a Sunday. Well, actually, we are not really allowed to use it but we have never been caught in twenty years so we are not about to stop now. Last week Tom opened all the doors to the outside cold to create a giant steam bath. They were like two lone Jigokudani Snow Monkeys. Brilliant.

I have to admit that swimming is not a pastime that I am missing particularly. I am a weak swimmer at best. This would not really be a problem if not for the ironic fact that I have given birth to a dolphin daughter. Pretty much from month one Emily has had a scary affinity with water, specifically, being under the water. This has given me one or two interesting moments over the years.

When I took her to the Mother and Baby beginner swimming lessons and it came to the big one where you submerge your precious, terrified baby under water, Emily came back up screaming her head off. Not, as the lovely instructor lady thought, because she has just been dunked, but rather because she hadn't been dunked deep or long enough.

Another time, when Emily was about four, a lady who I didn’t know suddenly dived into the water and pulled Emily out of the water screaming, “Your baby’s drowning! Your baby's drowning!" No matter how much I tried to explain that Emily was actually practicing the fine art of 'mushrooming' which involves lying stock still, legs and arms outstretched and face down in the water to see how long you can float for, her lady rescuer was having none of it. Ok, mushrooming does look remarkably like drowning but I was only half a foot away, how much of a useless Mother did she take me to be?

Over the years as Emily has got stronger, bigger and more frightening in the water, her favourite pastime is to create torture sessions, sorry, I mean games for us to play. Thankfully, as Emily has grown to understand, and to tolerate my ineptitude in the water, most of these games involve her Dad rather than me. Thank God. Tom is a really strong swimmer, and I think and hope that he enjoys these games as much as Emily. I hope so as there is no back up after Tom. The theme that runs through all of these games is brutality, pain and rules THAT MUST BE ADHERED TO AT ALL TIMES. 'I demand the diamond (pronounced D-I-MOND!) is one such favourite. It originated in a Tenerife swimming pool that was rapidly losing its floor tiles. Once a tile had been captured the game could begin. The first stage was to lob the 'd-i-mond' as far as possible, preferably into the darkest, deepest, coldest part of the pool. The second stage was then to get the d-i-mond back first while preventing your fellow d-i-mond hunter from getting there alive and before you. In order to achieve this, nothing, I mean, nothing is off limits; yanking, thumping, pulling, gouging, scratching, biting, drowning. And when you are victorious and lift the precious d-i-mond? It all starts again. This game is utterly exhausting to watch never mind play. Some of the more famous bouts have lasted over three hours. Three hours! Safe to say I have yet to receive an invite to join in this game. Thank The Lord.

Unfortunately, there are two games that Emily does require my participation in. The first is called 'Mum and Daughter Mermaids.' Ok, this doesn't sound too bad. Swimming calmly round the pool looking for coral reefs and good looking mer-mans? WRONG! These mermaids are hard core and are not remotely interested in mer-men. And of course there are plenty of rules. First one being these mermaids MUST swim along the bottom of the pool AT ALL TIMES! I can't even get to the bottom of the pool never mind about stay there. Second rule; legs must be kept together for authenticity AT ALL TIMES! Again, I am in deep trouble here. My only method of moving in the water is breast stroke; if I keep my legs together I don't go anywhere. Third rule, and perhaps the scariest, is that YOU MUST do a triple somersault after every three whips of your tail if you want to be a real mermaid. And finally, on NO account must you come up for air as mermaids don't need air to survive, apparently. Well I do, approximately 30 seconds after being deprived of it. Safe to say I fall slightly below Emily's standards of a Mum Mermaid.

The second game that Tom gets a get out of jail free card for on the account that he has testicles and wants to keep them is 'Butt Waves.' Again, this originated in Tenerife and keeps the tradition of self-harm and brutality alive and well. Ideally it is 'played' in the roughest and cruellest Atlantic beaches for maximum fear factor. The game involves sitting on your butt in the most dangerous death zone of the incoming tide - the place where the waves break and the undertow drags; the place that all the sensible people who don't have masochistic daughters avoid. The aim is to remain in the same position pre killer wave as post killer wave. This is not what happens to me. Ever. Emily seems to be able to keep a low sense of gravity or she has a particularly grippy back-side. I, on the other hand, am destroyed spectacularly by each and every wave. Firstly, I take the full facial impact of the white wave as it crashes over my head. My pathetic body is then picked up, usually by my toes and hurled up the beach – just for a brief moment I always think it might turn out all right at this point- but it never does. I am then slam dunked un-ceremoniously face down on the sand and finally dragged at high speed back down the beach leaving most of my skin on the hard basalt rocks, while my bikini bottoms float off somewhere out to La Palma. Gasping for air and dignity I resume my place back next to Emily who hasn't moved an inch. "You're not bored yet, Mum, are you?" she asks innocently. God no. I once played butt waves with Emily for over two hours. I hit the wall and went right through it. I had lost all feeling in my back side and all down my front and was so cold the rest of me was totally numb. I actually went weirdly euphoric and started screaming at the waves, “Is that all you've got! Come to Mamma! You can't shift my butt!” I'm not proud.

I am sure my lacklustre love of the water stems from my childhood swimming lessons. After my Mum had finally dragged me kicking and screaming from the inside of my beautiful rainbow rubber ring where I had been cowering for seven years and showed me that I would actually have to get wet below the middle in order to be able to swim, my sister and I had to suffer primary school swimming lessons. Every Monday we would take the cold and hideous walk down the hill from school to pool, get changed in the cold and hideous changing rooms, shrivel into the cold and hideous public swimming baths and wait to be shouted at by the cold and hideous Mrs Laidlaw. The only thing that Mrs Laidlaw despised more than children was children who couldn't swim. She didn't like me at all. She always wore a hideous black swimming costume despite being a healthy sixteen plus stone and never once going anywhere near the water in all the years she taught us. I say taught. Her methods were a bit similar to the method of letting a child cry in order to learn how to go to sleep. It will be mighty painful but will probably work in the end. We basically just swam round and round and round and round and round and round the pool until we started to sink, either from exhaustion or just a lack of wanting to live any more. At this point the lovely Mrs Laidlaw used to grab one of those long poles with a little hook on the end, used to pull open high up Victorian windows, and drag us out by our costumes. She also used this weapon to herd back into the side any errant child who had dared to cut a corner while on his or her 75th lap of the pool. It worked though. From our first half-walking, half-lurching five metres, to the more serious five hundred metres and then the holy grail fifteen hundred metres, we all learnt to swim, a very long way. And what did we get for all our hard work? A sew on cloth badge that our parents, oh so loved to sew on to our costumes of an evening and we, oh so, loved to slowly pick off our costumes so it created a lovely pocket for water to hide in and act as mini weights round our sides. Just to make swimming that little bit more pleasurable.

And then there is 'knickergate'. That fateful day. My sister and I must have been trying clothes on before school because for some reason I decided to put my swimming costume on under my school uniform and left my knickers at home. I only realised this problematic fact when I came to get changed after swimming. "Er, I don't suppose anyone has a spare pair of pants do they?" I embarrassingly whispered from my cubicle. Strangely, and to this day I will never know why, someone piped up, "Yes, I do" and a perfectly serviceable pair of grey knickers came whizzing over the top of my door. No questions asked I was good to go and thought nothing more of it. Until, that was, my

Mother appeared at the classroom door later that morning. Now, I am not sure whether, over the years, I have added character to my Mum's actions here, or she did indeed march straight in to the front of the class holding high and proud a pair of yellow knickers for everyone to see. "Lucy left these at home this morning!" she announced to a chorus of titters and giggles. "My God!" my lovely teacher exclaimed, "It must have been mighty drafty for you up that hill, Lucy!" What could I do? Explain that I was in fact wearing someone's (I didn't know who) spare?/only? pair of pants and was perfectly snug or pretend that yes indeed I was thankful for my not-embarrassing-at-all-Mum for rescuing me from fanny frost bite. In the event I can't remember the next hour or two. I think I have blanked it from my memory. I may even have ended up wearing two pairs of knickers for the remainder of the day. Who knows?

Safe to say water and me have some bad history. Mind you, now that my hair is rapidly falling out all over my body, perhaps my new Goodhew-esque finish gives me a small window of opportunity to up my game and become the Mermaid Mum Emily has always dreamed I could be. Or not.

Chapter 54.

Ding Dong: Round Two

I probably have to admit that I have lost round one to chemo. Not a knock out but definitely a loss on points. Two infections, three days in hospital and six days in bed is not the greatest performance; five to go, though, so plenty of opportunity to show better form.

That's if it goes ahead as scheduled. I have to have my bloods done for the millionth time today to check whether I am back in double figures. If my remaining red and/or white blood cells have thrown in the white (or red) towel then it gets postponed until my immunity has recovered. I feel excellent today so I am confident I will be ready to take a few more punches tomorrow.

A beautiful sunny, blue skied today; perfect for a long walk and some much needed fresh air. That is after I escape from the hospital. Getting your bloods done at hospital is an interesting experience. Upon declaring your presence, you are invited to take ownership of a little pink, numbered ticket; number 51 for me. It's the same machine and appears to be the same system used at supermarket delis to avoid a punch up over the last slice of smoked ham. We all sit, strangely, facing the wall with our backs to the receptionist who is on calling duty. Maybe it is to add to the suspense of waiting for your special number to be called out, I don't know.

"Thirty-seven!" Bloody hell! Ten minutes per patient, times fourteen! 10 x 14 = a long wait facing the wall when I want to be in the winter sunshine. But what do you know? The next number called is forty-six. Ok? Some patients must have lost the will to live and done a runner. Who cares, not so long to wait now. "Number fifty-four!" What the hell? What happened to fifty-one? And all the other numbers between thirty-seven and forty-six and fifty-four for that matter? This wasn't a ticket system it was a bloody raffle, with no prizes.

I never win anything at raffles or tombolas for that matter. Ever. No matter how crap or strange the prizes, I never get the tickets ending in five of zero no matter how many I buy. What always happens is I go from not caring at all; knowing that, strangely my life will not be improved by being the proud owner of a hideous green and yellow home-made pottery vase, to really, really wanting to be the proud owner of a hideous green yellow home-made pottery vase. And the 1500-piece jigsaw of a twee winter scene that someone has written, 'No pieces missing!' in biro on the front of. And the single bar of Imperial Leather soap. Or the knit your own hot water bottle kit. And especially the only half decent prize on show; the bottle of Blue Nun. Which suspiciously has the only yellow ticket on it whose counterpart everyone knows won't even be added until there are only two prizes left. I want them all really, really badly.

They could cheer up proceedings at the hospital a great deal if they combined the two ticket systems and added in an Xmas tombola. Just imagine; pick the winning ticket and not only could you be waiting for less than two hours before you meet the needle lady you could also be the proud owner of a 2015 Cliff Richard Calendar. Perfect.

Chapter 55.

Chicken Feet

We went for a Chinese meal today. A good Boxing Day antidote to all things Christmas while keeping the theme of over eating alive and well.

One of the most ridiculous and over the top Chinese restaurants I have ever been to was in my halogen days as Senior Condiments and Cooking Sauces Buyer (no less) at Asda. My team and I were regularly wined, dined and bribed by suppliers whose dreams of expanding their chutney empires via my shelves could only be realised by taking us out for ostentatious meals. We had no complaints.

This particular Chinese restaurant was in Mayfair and had three menus; one listing the food, one listing the wine and the third listing the prices of the extremely fine and expensive Chinese artwork for sale in glass cabinets adorning the walls. All the tables were vast banquet spheres with mesmeric spinning turntables atop more complex spinning tables. They looked like a pre-Socrates view of lots of earths spinning in their galaxies. So of course a bunch of stupid twenty somethings prime entertainment was to spin these planets as fast as we could to see whether Szechuan duck could indeed defy centrifugal gravity.

It is apt that I can't remember the name of this restaurant, any of the dishes I ate, or whether my lovely supplier actually ended up with a chutney listing. I do remember, however, that the bill for sixteen of us came (to our glee and the suppliers' horror) to just under two grand; very silly.

At the other, preferable in my view, end of the Chinese Restaurant scale is Ho's. Named, not as we speculated, as a homage to prostitutes, or a subtle nod to Christmas (especially if they had opened a sister and brother outlet either side), but rather more simply and sensibly after the owner, Mr Ho.

There are a number of essential characteristics to a fine and genuine not-interested-in-catering-for-stupid-English-people-Chinese Restaurant. The first is the ambience. This must be somewhere between bus depot and front room. There must be a faint smell of something undisclosed and a slight dampness created by years of endlessly steaming pork and prawn dumplings. There must be no table cloths. All tables must be covered in sheets of pink and white paper pulled generously from a large roller in the centre of the restaurant. Ideally, there will be a large number of laminated signs posted unnecessarily on all of the walls. Thoughtfully ensuring that we know where the toilets are, and are not, at every turn, and where the kitchens are, and the front door and the back door and so on. Finally, and this is the best sign to witness, the restaurant should be packed with only Chinese consumers; seriously, quietly, expertly and at mind boggling speed, eating, and eating and eating.

I have only ever seen two gatherings of Chinese friends and families at Ho's. The first group are the banquet families. If you are able you will count approximately seventy-two family members over three, possibly four, maybe even five generations. From aged one to a hundred and one, all ages will defy any preconceptions of how much it is possible to eat at this age. As the meal advances at least five or six babies will be lost for some hours under the weight of bowls of noodles as the table disappears under the sheer volume of dishes which never stop arriving through the length of the meal. There are no tantrums and demands for chicken nuggets and chips from these children. They can see their forefathers across the table from them still going strong at least a hundred years on. This is serious. There's no time to be fussy they need to pay attention. They know they are in training for they have much to learn.

The second groups are always students; girls and boys that look like they haven't had a decent Chinese meal since primary school, and they are now intent on making up for it. Amazingly they manage to consume at bullet train speed while at the same time talking non-stop and texting and phoning all at the same time.

And then there is the Verinder's. We have earned the right to be here too. We know the unspoken rules; quantity and speed. And no namby-pamby spoons or forks required. We are no amateur speedsters. Chop sticks banged on the table three times to signal the battle has commenced and we are off. And it is by no means a fair battle. We all have our tried and tested tactics to achieve gluttony. Emily's is surprisingly advanced and clever given the relatively short time she has been consuming Chinese Food. I call it the 'cordon'. What she does is proclaim certain of her favourite dishes as exclusively hers (which Tom and I strangely accept) and cordons them off into her own eating space and bans any other family member from sharing. Egg fried rice x 2 portions – cordoned. Steamed prawn dumplings – cordoned. To this day I have never tasted a steamed prawn dumpling. I wouldn't dare. However, having designated her own monster private meal, Emily does not allow the same treatment to be given by anyone else for any of the other dishes. Oh no, these are all proclaimed municipal. Deep fried cuttle fish – municipal. BBQ spare ribs – municipal. Furthermore, municipal dishes are consumed before cordoned dishes which are then enjoyed latterly and at leisure only by Emily. Brilliant.

Tom's tactics are no less devious. Tom aims for superior gluttony by ordering dishes that he knows Emily and I will be too frightened of to eat. These dishes tend to be either extreme entrails or extreme internal parts. They usually have claws and/or tendrils and usually glow glutinously. These dishes look like they are more likely to up sticks and consume you than the other way round. Tom is totally confident that he has at least these dishes exclusively to himself. It is very clever.

And my genius tactic? Mine is definitely less advanced but no less effective for it. I just eat at warp speed hoovering up as quickly as humanly possible everything in front of me. No real tactic just greed.

All of the above means that our Chinese Meals usually last no more than twenty-three minutes. It normally takes us longer to drive, park and walk to Ho's than eat at Ho's. Our fellow consumers aren't even quarter of the way through their meals and we are asking for the bill.

But not before the second coming.

The second coming is unique to Chinese Food. Without exception, this never happens at any other type of restaurant. It takes place approximately ten minutes after the first ending of the meal when you sit back absolutely stuffed and slightly sickened by the fatty, deep fried left overs in front of you. Despite the sheer volume eaten, it is guaranteed that there will be some leftovers. This is because the English eye is always so much bigger than the Chinese stomach. But now, suddenly, that spare rib glowing Aztec red in its own fatty juices, that ten minutes ago you knew, if you ate, would take you to the edge of Creosote territory, looks quite appetising. Similarly, the last remnants of duck meat clinging to that leg bone absolutely must be rolled into one more wafer thin Peking duck wrap. This phenomenon is probably because we have consumed so much salt, sugar and monosodium glutamate that our livers have packed up and our taste buds just don't care anymore.

Either way, I am an expert at the second coming. It is usually where I steal a late win in the gluttony battle. In fact, today, as I am still playing catch up on the food front due to the last few pitiful weeks, I actually made it to an unprecedented third coming and Tom had to virtually drag me by my coat hood out of the restaurant. I bloody love Christmas.

Chapter 56.

Bitter Sweet Symphony

Emily and I went to Leeds White Rose shopping centre today; a well overdue Mum and Daughter shopping session. Over the years, without really realising it, we have developed a strict itinerary that we never deviate from, ever.

First stop; car park 2, so we can walk through Primark. Not to shop but to play the Primark game. The game is influenced by Richard Ashcroft's infamous walk in the Verve video for Bitter Sweet Symphony. You remember the one; where he nonchalantly walks along a busy street singing into the camera and knocking aside anyone or anything that gets in his way without so much as a flinch. That is what Emily and I must do. The winner is the one that can make it across the vast, chaotic store from one door to the other in a straight line, without being beaten up by an aggrieved Indian grandmother armed with seven pairs of stilettos. To my delight I won today as Emily got side-tracked by a pair of Garfield pyjamas.

I am slightly scared of Primark. For someone with low lying OCD, the shop tends to bring me out in a light sweat. I think it's due to the fact that the shop and its customers are constantly engaged in the pursuit of quantity over quality; it has the permanent atmosphere of a manic January Sale day. The place is always an utter tip. The depressed shop assistants have all given up ages ago at any vague attempt to fold or correctly hang any of the clothes on hangers. Generally, they are just piled precariously high on numerous tables for people to wrestle and fight over and stuff victoriously into their ever expanding net shopping baskets. It is all very depressing. It is our fault that shops like this exist. We have spawned these emporiums of mass produced tat. They are only supplying to our greedy obsessions of want over need and getting away with it due to the fact that we appear to easily be able to turn a blind eye to the horrible impact up and down the supply chain; having said that, I do really like their bed socks.

Next stop; Build-A-Bear. Emily always enters this shop with a mixture of embarrassment and joy. Embarrassment because, as an achingly cool, style conscious, eleven-year-old, she still loves and adores all things Build-A-Bear. And joy because as an achingly cool, style conscious eleven-year-old she still loves and adores all things Build-A-Bear. After a quick scan to make sure no-one she knows is in the shop she gleefully sets about seeing whether there is anything on sale that she doesn't already own. Our Build-A-Bear experience is no doubt the same as millions of other parents. It started, innocently enough, about seven years ago when we had fairly healthy bank balances. Step one; your adored little precious one selects a pathetic, sad looking unstuffed bear from a dump bin, purposefully designed to make them look woeful and un-loved. Once said bear is selected the magic (clever con) begins. You are taken over to the 'stuffing machine' that looks like something out of Willy Wonker's factory. One of the many disturbingly happy staff (they have hideous uniform and have to wear strange Build-A-Bear back packs) greets you gleefully and invites your child to press the start button that sends the stuffing up a tube and into your bear. A quick series of skilful stitches down its back and it has been transformed from a mass produced £10 flat packed anonymous bear into the creature that will over the next half century systematically fleece you of half your income. This is because Build-A-Bears have their own individual Birth Certificates which obviously means that they cannot remain naked; they are virtually human for God's sake. And here is the rub. While this sweet little bear is a fairly reasonable £10 naked, donned in a pair of pink sequined trousers, the little sod immediately doubles in price. Plus, it doesn't stop at clothes; this little fucker demands sun glasses, a bed, roller skates, a winter coat, Xmas jumpers, a Halloween outfit. It goes on. To top it all you can actually purchase a Bear for your Build-A-Bear and, yes, Build-A-Bear Bears need clothing. Emily's bear has more, beautifully designed outfits for all occasions than her entire extended family put together.

Next stop is always Paper Chase. Emily has inherited my slightly strange love of all things stationery. I still, sadly, remember the joy of purchasing pencil cases full of goodies required for the start of a new school term. A virginal WHSmith white tablet rubber did things to me that perhaps was not entirely natural. Paper Chase is very clever. It designs themes for all its collections so that once a skull festooned pencil case has been fallen in love with, there is absolutely no way the shop can be left without purchasing matching pencils, files, note pads and even iPhone cover. And the next time you pop in to add an A4 pad to your in sync collection? All obsolete. Obviously. But there is a gorgeous funky rose patterned A4 pad to die for – and matching pencil case, etc. I know what is happening but am seemingly powerless to do anything about it.

Final stop before lunch; SuperDry. I love this dark shop of delights. The clothes are on the whole pretty unimaginatively designed casual hoodies and t-shirts made glorious (and very expensive) with the crazy addition of a bright orange label and day-go bright pink SuperDry moniker. That's it, really. I was feeling crazy so I bought a woolly blue bobble hat; made expensive and glorious due to a bright orange label and pink SuperDry moniker across the front. Gorgeous. SuperDry is one of those shops that leaves me with an afterglow. I feel, for at least ten or fifteen minutes upon departure the possibility of youthful coolness infiltrating me via my bald head. I have even learnt the correct hipster angle to wear my hats, to Emily's visible relief.

Lunch is always Handmade Burger and we always have exactly the same meal. Emily loves this place primarily because I allow her to have a chocolate milkshake BEFORE her burger and for the 'bottomless' drinks. In the same way as on an all-inclusive holiday, despite the fact that you have more than paid for all the drinks upfront you are now consuming; the fact that you can have as many as you want, now makes you inhumanly thirsty. Emily can consume multiple Pepsis in Handmade Burger, whereas in most restaurants and pubs she struggles to finish one. Everything about the way this place markets itself is designed to distance itself as far as possible in its customers' minds from McDonalds. It does this by telling you at every point possible that its burgers are handmade – yes, we've got it, from scratch, from prime Scottish Beef. All good stuff but I am sure they could have done a bit better than the strap line, 'Making burgers from scratch since 2006'. There are a couple of things that don't quite send the heart souring with this statement. Firstly, if you are going to show off about how long you have been doing something, to impress the punter it usually has to be a bit longer than 10 years. 1888, may be, or 1910 but not 2006, it really isn't that long. Secondly making something from scratch sounds too like making something from scraps. Lastly, aren't all burgers handmade? Surely the important bit is handmade with what? McDonald's burgers can claim to come in contact with hands; it is the 99 percent bread, water, salt, one percent cow hoof content that worries me. That said, Handmade Burger Co. is good fast food and at least while Emily is eating she is not purchasing anything.

After food we are always too full to shop anymore; home time and time for the Visa to cool down.

On reflection, maybe a few more bouts of sickness wouldn't be a bad thing if it keeps my daughter away from retail heaven.

Chapter 57.

Black Star

What is there left to write? There are pages and pages of printed press. National papers wrapping their daily news in iconic images and song lyrics; whole arts sections given over to journalists retelling the time they met him in 2002 for 6 minutes. Endless tenuous claims to friendship and genuine tales of heart rending fan-based love; everyone trying desperately to do the same thing; place their own, small, mundane, earth based lives somewhere of importance next to the vast, wondrous, weird greatness that is/was David Bowie.

I loved him retrospectively at first. 'Low'. 'Heroes'. 'Lodger'. Catching up on his music from the decade I was born. I finally got alongside him in the 80's. "Let's Dance. Put on your red shoes and dance the blues." I mean, COME ON!!! The dirty sexiness of China Girl. "She says, ssssshhhhh, just shut your mouth." Mmm. Hated by his achingly cool Ziggy fans, loved by millions. Even in the 90's and into the 21st century I always had a Bowie song warm from repeated listening somewhere high up on my play list. 'Thursday's Child' from 'Hours'. 'Where are we now?' from 'The Next Day'.

An ever-growing number of years passed in-between albums. To me he was like having a super cool, unfaithful best friend. A total delight to be around but you knew he would fuck off and leave you as soon as the really cool party started somewhere else and he wouldn't invite you. Left to your much more boring non-Bowie-lit life you swore to reject him next time he condescended to return and give you some attention. His music was shit anyway; over indulgent, theatrical, pretentious. And then he would return, with his devilish grin and dangerous black shot eye. And that voice. And you were hooked in again. Damn him. Love him.

And then he died.

The total bastard came back and gave me 'Black Star' on Friday and then fucked off and died on Sunday. Shit. The "I'm dying to………" of 'Dollar Days' had two o's not one.

And, despite all that has been written over the last few days, all the sadness, all the shock, not one person has mentioned the real truth about what we are feeling. FEAR. We are really frightened. Frightened because David Bowie was meant to live forever; David Bowie was meant to outlive us all. He was meant to write new albums for my daughter too when she was in her 40's, in 2045. He was certainly not meant to die of cancer that, oh so, earthly, boring, incurable disease. We are frightened because while Mr Bowie was eternal he was proof that there was life on Mars. He was proof that there was a God and he loves us. He was proof that you can do whatever you want to do; be anyone, or anything, you want to be. He virtually singlehandedly brought down the Berlin wall for Christ sake! Proof that life is incredible. Now he's gone we are not so sure any more.

Chapter 58.

Get back out there! BE BOLD AND BRAVE, GIRL!

These were the words of Emily's netball teacher during half time. They were directed at Emily with astonishing, and frankly frightening, belief and passion. Emily's netball teacher does not believe, on any level, that she is *just* coaching a bunch of pre-pubescent under twelve girls who, let's be honest would probably rather be at home of a Saturday morning eating toast and watching YouTube. Tune in young ladies. Listen up.

PUT YOUR CYNICISM ASIDE RIGHT NOW! Netball is the single greatest sport in the world! You, girls, are the greatest sporting prodigies of your age! This second half performance could change your lives!

It didn't, unfortunately.

They lost 18 – 6. Emily and her team are not yet quite tuned in to their teacher's unique wave length. Their heads had already dropped by half time. Their fragile egos had already crumbled. They hated netball with a passion; now and forever.

I, on the other hand was pumped. I was totally tuned in; give me a touch line coach over calm, crowd-side containment any day. Give me a Mourinho over a van Gaal. Give me a heart on a sleeve over a tight lip. Give me an enthusiastic hug over a limp handshake; any day. While her girls let her down, I was her star pupil. Running up and down the touch line, arms pumping, fingers pointing, imaginary whistle blowing.

I expended more energy than Emily's whole team put together. I got recruited on the spot. Not as Wing Attack (shame, I would have been delighted) but as her Tuesday after school deputy coach.

Today Silcoates school under 12's, tomorrow England! COME ON!

Get back out there! BE BOLD AND BRAVE, GIRL!

………………………………………………………………

………………………………………………………………

My chemo treatment had also dragged itself to half-time today. I didn't get any orange halves or motivating pep talks. 9 weeks in and 9 weeks to go (if I include 3 weeks of Radiotherapy.) It's safe to say I could have done with a bit of both. Ironically it's World Cancer Awareness Day; a perfect day to spend seven and half hours in hospital having chemotherapy. Not! I have noticed a growing number of column inches on the subject of cancer over the last few weeks. In addition to the continuous sensationalist headlines about advances in treatment that are always suspiciously not so imminent sounding in the small print, two articles have stood out.

The first riled me. An eminent female Dr (I don't remember her name) had caused a stir by claiming a direct link with breast cancer and drinking too much red wine. She clearly had not stopped to think how that might make those of us who like a drink (or two) and have had breast cancer, feel. Further, the supercilious cow, had congratulated herself personally for being cancer free, which she put directly down to her having displayed the will power and intelligence to abstain from the nightly temptations of a glass of vino. Thus, by association, suggesting that I was not just unlucky, as I had thought, but actually stupid, alcoholic and weak willed. Well, lady, let me tell you something; when, in 30 years you are inevitably still alive living your long and correct life, and still nightly patting yourself on the back as you sip your dull glass of water, I might *not* still be alive but my time on earth will have been considerably more fun packed, and wine filled than yours, you pompous, insulting cow.

The second article that caught my eye was about a young lady who had had the post of her naked breast taken down by Facebook. She had posted it to show as many women as possible what to look out for in rarer forms of cancer. Aside from being impressed with her brilliance (she was terminal) it was a curt reminder that however powerful and personal we believe our FT posts to be, in reality they are simply seen by the FB machine as corporate fodder. My over-arching thought, though was;

Get back out there! BE BOLD AND BRAVE, GIRL!

Chapter 59.

The Return of the She Boiler

It's actually happened. Who could ever have imagined it? All the time the She Boiler had spent under the stairs in the dark with my innocent looking washing machine, they had been colluding; hatching a plan for revenge. Safely deposited in the local skip I had thought I was free of her wicked ways but it turns out not to be the case. I, unlike the majority of people, don't believe domestic white goods are inanimate objects. The She Boiler is clear evidence of this. To add strength to my argument I now have the washing machine and I have always had the dishwasher. This is why. When the dishwasher finishes its perfectly precise cycle it (no, let's call her a she), she beeps. This is not a quiet, pleasant beep, asking you politely, if it is convenient, that is, to open the door to aid the cooling process. No, this is a rude, alarming and ear splitting BEEP!!! And she doesn't beep once, oh no, she beeps seven times, BEEP!!! BEEP!!! BEEP!!! BEEP!!! BEEP!!! BEEP!!! BEEP!!! The timing of this beep will never, ever coincide with you being in the kitchen; ever. Usually we are in bed. Just. Yes, we can hear her from the other side of the house. Worse, she doesn't do her BEEP x 7 once and remain quiet for the rest of the night. She will wait approximately seven more minutes before repeating her demands. Seven minutes is precisely the time required to ensure we have forgotten about her and been lulled into a peaceful sleep. It is not, however, long enough for the BEEP!! not to annoy to a greater level, so soon after the previous BEEP!!! Obviously, now we are riled, so to show her who is boss we won't go down stairs to open her door we will leave her to BEEP!!! and proceed to forget about her and then be furious when she goes off again. And so on………….. This battle can last through the night with neither side giving in. And I have had a further thought. Why does her door need to be opened at the end of the fucking cycle anyway? I know enough about science to know that water dries and hot things cool all in good time. Are my pots and plates *really* going to incinerate if they are left incarcerated?

I digress to prove a point. Back to the She Boiler and the Traitor Washing Machine. The plot they had hatched together was a clever dish served cold.

Stage 1: Wait until the new boiler was settled in and working like a dream so that the She Boiler was a distant memory.

Stage 2: Traitor Washing Machine breaks. Cleverly trap an errant sweater's arm in the door and proceed to spin it into a twisted rope long and strong enough to pull a boat in troubled water, and in the process rip the rubber seal round the door, and therefore ingeniously create a full bore waterfall feature down the wrong side of the door.

Stage 3: While being fixed by the engineer ensure that the mains water supply is not turned off correctly so that a jettison of water explodes all over the boiler and into the floor boards and pipes.

Stage 4: Said flood ensures that the thermostat short circuits and dies.

Stage 5: Wonderful 21st Century Boiler is now retro-boiler, capable only of being switched off; no hot water and no heating. And switched on; hot water at scalding temperature only and radiators that melt the walls.

Remind you of anybody?

As I passed through the hall this morning I swear the hairs stood up on the back of my neck and I saw through the corner of my eye a cold, white ghostly shadow.

Chapter 60.

Coffee v Tea

I am a tea drinker now. In a past life I was a coffee lover. Coffee is a booster. Tea is a soother. I used to need a boost; one in the morning to get my eyes open at 6.45am and legs out of bed. One from the machine at work to get my brain sparking for the first meeting and one midafternoon to get me through the afternoon drag and lag. I was never a caffeine addict; unlike some colleagues at work, with their daily lipstick-smeared drive through, Costa Coffee Cappuccinos wrapped in shaking hands before the 8 o'clock meeting. Always a bit concerning, especially when followed by the can of coke chaser.

Now I need soothing and tea is an unexplored loveliness. I have graduated from the impatient dunking of the tea bag in the mug, jabbed with a tea spoon and then chucked in the sink. Now I have a twin set of beautiful stainless steel tea pots; one very cute diddy one which produces tea for one and a bit, and a grand sociable one that makes tea for two thousand.

It is not possible to pour a cup of tea without feeling fine and even perhaps a bit sophisticated. I don't find it possible not to go 'aaaahhh' when I drink the first sip or not to wrap my hands round the warming mug and wish for a dunking biscuit. Goodbye to rush hour coffee and hello to contemplative tea.

Tailors of Harrogate, Yorkshire Leaf Tea only, of course. Let's have a proper brew.

Chapter 61.

Top 10 tips to get the school run done on time

1. If your child is of homework age do not raise the subject of homework in the morning, in any form whatsoever. If your child *has* completed his/her nightly dose, then asking whether they have done their homework, will be a deeply insulting indictment of their maturity and ability to work independently; and further prove, as a parent that you don't respect or understand how they feel/think/act etc. If they *haven't* done their homework a meltdown will ensue that will only slow proceedings down further with no time to complete said homework anyway.

2. No-one is going to see, or enter, your house during the day, except, perhaps you, so there is no need to start to try and tidy the resulting mess of morning madness before you leave. For example, deciding to clean behind the toaster is not necessary. More than a life time of toast crumbs will be hiding there, ready to scatter excessively over your surface tops. Leave well alone.

3. Do not decide to clean everyone's shoes to compensate for lateness; especially not with your never previously used Lord Sheridan Premium Shoe Cleaning Kit, there is no time. If you really can't resist then spit, kitchen roll and the back of your hand will suffice.

4. Again, on icy mornings, do not suddenly decide that you will finally put your 5 stage premium deicer car kit to the test that has been locked in the glove compartment since 2010. This is not the time. Take a kettle full of suitably cooled water and chuck it round the car. Get in quickly, try not to breathe and get the windscreen wipers on, preferably before the water re-freezes.

5. Being woken up early and un-naturally by an alarm clock can never be turned into a pleasant experience; face into it. Setting your alarm half an hour earlier to a more soothing and only gradually alarming wakeup call will not work. It will only result in 30 minutes of a suspended half sleep, half stressful state, where you will imagine that you have jumped joyfully out of bed and are now singing tunefully in the shower whereas in fact your face is still spit glued to the pillow and you haven't moved an inch. Change the plan. Set you alarm 30 minutes later than required, as loud as possible, to the most pycho-esque alarm sound that you can find. The resulting shock when woken, together with the realization that you are now horribly late, will be painful, yes, but will also generate a hugely convenient adrenalin rush that will jolt you out of bed wired and now able to get a shift on.

6. If you have a girl (or girls) now is the time to introduce them to the power of female multitasking. The only skill that will get them through life, break the glass ceilings, and enable them to power ahead of their male counterparts at school and in the future;

apparently. For now, that means that it is indeed possible to put your shirt and blazer on at the *same time* as brushing your teeth *and* combing your hair. It can be done.

7. Breakfast. Set the breakfast table the previous night. Come down stairs early to start hand preparing croissants and your own homemade jam, freshly squeezed orange juice and ethically ground coffee. Call everyone to the table and proceed to consume while engaging in enlightening and insightful conversation with all the family. OR……… ask once what they want for breakfast. If the answer is "nothing", then leave it at that; if it is affirmative, offer only quick fire cereal or at a push, toast. Provide it by the TV, don't expect a thank you before 8 o'clock and finish any remains as your own breakfast. Jobs a good 'un.

8. If the white shirt ironing requirement in your house is into double figures every week congratulate yourself on even getting close to keeping up. Monday, Tuesday and possibly even Wednesday is a good performance. On a slack week fold down collars and scrub any obvious marks that can't be covered by a tie with a multi – wipe. Remaining options are to take a stand on the drudgery of ironing and just refuse point blank to do it. Or show your family how a crumpled shirt hung in a warm damp bathroom overnight will be perfectly good to go in the morning.

9. Drop off is just that; *Drop Off*. If your child/ children is/are still at an age where they adore you and don't want to leave you and need long, deep hugs of

affection before the painful parting, enjoy it but don't indulge it. It won't last. If your child/children now can't get away from you fast enough don't pine for the days when they adored you and didn't want to leave you and needed long, deep hugs of affection. Be cool. They probably do still quite like you in their own secret way.

10. Get an illness that allows you to lie warm and snuggled up in bed until at least 10.30 every morning so you don' t have to worry about any of the above.

Chapter 62.

Poached Egg Flower

My twin sister lives in Sydney, Australia. This, it has not gone unnoticed by us both, is as physically far apart as two sisters can possibly be. It's not ideal but it is also brilliant in many unique ways. One of the first things my nurse said to me upon diagnosis was that it is a myth that only bad things come out of bad things. Often putting the brakes on your life and changing course, forced or otherwise, and having the time to see things properly, is a great thing.

My sister sends me photographs on WhatsApp of close-ups of flowers that she has seen on her way to work, or out and about. I like to think of her stopping and taking the time to snap their uniqueness just for me. Some of the flowers catch her eye only if they have an uncanny resemblance to something un-flower-like. A beautiful white flower that looks like a perfectly fragile poached egg; a hilarious looking, proudly upright fuzzy flower that looks remarkably like a loo brush; a fluffy yellow happy fat flower that looks just like a tennis ball. Perfect.

Chapter 63.

Tull v Waits

Music is a must for me. From vinyl and tapes, to CDs and iPod, to blue toothed Bose and streamed Spotify; it doesn't matter as long as it's there. Tom and I have a large mutual music memory bank built up over the years. It doesn't have quite the same deposits; me: Folk; Tom: Blues but there is plenty of shared investment. And we have a game. Often played of an evening when Tom has finally got fed up with me playing my 'latest finds'. It's called 'pass the song' and the rules are simple. One of you selects a song. You both listen. Then the other one selects a song, linked in some way to the previous song, then repeat. Simple, silly and soppy, perhaps, but frankly who cares.

The game is pretty formulaic. We always start on common ground with the safe, greats; Bob, Leonard, Van the Man. Mixed with a sprinkling of the Nick's; Cave and Drake, and then move on to the vast collection of depressing, male singer song writers; Ed Harcourt, Tom McCrae, Andrew Bird, etc., etc,………………

And then it happens. Always around the same time; I just can't help it. I think, is he ready? I've buttered him up with a bit of Bowie? Maybe this time he will see the light?

IT'S TULL TIME!!! Jethro Tull! the greatest, single living rock band on earth, in my humble opinion.

If I link them in lightly with a more bluesy track; 'Wond'rin Aloud', maybe, or 'Life's A Long Song', Tom will finally catch their true poetic genius. Maybe he will be able to see that they are so much more than an ageing prog rock band whose lead singer has a passion for tight tights and cod pieces and likes to play his flute standing on one leg. The fucking flute! In a rock band! Jesus, Lucy, have you never considered why this has not caught on!!! How can you seriously write a song called, 'From a Dead Beat to an Old Greaser'? for God's sake!

Oh, well. It's very lonely loving 26 albums on your own, you know.

Meanwhile Tom is thinking; is it time? I've buttered her up with a bit of 'I am Kloot' maybe this time she's ready? Maybe this time she won't lynch me?

IT'S TOM TIME! The one and only freaky Tom Waits!

No it's fucking not! What the hell is this gravel - barreled theatrically meandering crap? He sounds like he's just resurrected himself from his own grave. Is he even in the same room as his musicians? Turn it off!

And so the game ends, every time. Not even the safe tuneful glue of Nick Drake can mend the gaping hole in our musical relationship. I go to bed with the scratching horrors of 'Nighthawk Postcards' ringing in my ears – 11 minutes 30 seconds long, for fucks sake! If you are going to be dreadful at least be quick about it. And Tom goes to bed hating Tull more than ever. Safe to say. 'Skating Away on the The Thin Ice of a New Day' did not move him as I had hoped.

There is always next time..........................

Chapter 64.

To Toss or Not to Toss

I can't cook. There we are; confessions of a 21st Century Woman. Don't cook. Won't cook. Can't cook. Frankly, who gives a..... I bring plenty to the Theatre of Marriage. Get over it.

Actually, I can cook. I can cook two things. One thing, if we are being picky and taking it back to source; batter. But I am short on numbers so let's call it two things.

I can cook Yorkshire puddings and I can make pancakes.

My skills in both these fields are legendary and unquestioned. Waiting eagerly in the wings of a Sunday afternoon, my culinary wizardry is essential to lift the roast to magical heights. My 'Yorkshires' don't give up the ghost half way through the bake, collapsing to resemble inedible 1930's soccer balls. Ever. Resplendent and monolithic my beauties rise confidently, well beyond their petite muffin bottoms, big enough to take up home in; without fail.

Pancakes are my second gift to the kitchen.

Not limited to Shrove Tuesday; any day can be Pancake Day. One egg some flour, water and milk and a pan is all that is required. Incredibly I can keep the recipe in my head. Pancakes are curious things. They share the spoils with oranges in having possibly the most uninspiring nominal name of all time. *Pan-Cake.*

They are made in a pan and they are round so let's call them pancakes! Genius. What about flip fritters? Or flying batter bombs? Contrary to popular belief pancakes are not actually that easy to make. The process is littered with fairly major potential disaster. Too much flour and you are closer to making a cake. Too much heat and you are scraping them into the bin. And decisions, decisions, what to top them with? In our house it's Nutella and Nutella only. Nutella, that curious childhood condiment that always tasted so fine on holiday French Baguettes but was always so woefully disappointing back home on Warburton's white. I can't imagine why.

And to the biggie; to toss or not to toss? Yes! Toss! Just like the 'tish' nose-holding sneezer, I am slightly suspicious of those afraid to let fly with the aaaaahhhh and the ooooooohhh!. The Italians do it. Happy to give air to everything; pizza bases, bread, spaghetti. But we are repressed by the French. *ZUT ALORS! Keep it in the pan, Monsieur!* Ok, there is less than 20% chance of the thing landing the required way up back in the pan but why flip the thing apologetically with the spatula when you can chuck it up in the air? And strangely, like two handed card shuffling and three-ball juggling, one handed pancake flipping elevates all practitioners to glory status. It just does. It's just cool to complete a perfect arc without mishap. You would find me in the kitchen a damn sight more often if it was de rigueur to chuck more food in the air as part of the cooking process. Boring Barnsley chops? No longer if half way through they required a nifty spin.

But for now I will limit myself to my brace of battered products.

Actually, thinking about it, *I could* extend my oeuvre to toad in the hole? How hard can it be? A dish with a proper name. AND I am sure the 'toads' would more than stand up to a spot of pan flipping.

Chapter 65.

Join me for a rum before breakfast

Tom is spending Valentine's Day in Europe's most romantic city; again. Not with me but with other people's teenage offspring. Do not underestimate the sheer time and skill required to plan, organise and execute a foreign school trip that runs with inspirational brilliance, every year, without fail. One of the reasons this trip is inspirational is because it merges French art, history, and language. I never understood why the A level cannons need walls. How can you learn about the French revolution without knowing and loving Delacroix' Liberty Leading the People? How can you really understand the meaning of David's Death of Marat without knowing about the life of the murdered French revolutionary leader? Can you change the way a young student thinks and feels forever, in 5 days, in Paris? Maybe.

This admirable annual pilgrimage to Paris, however, is fraught with potential pitfalls. Who would even dare take an academic trip abroad nowadays? The bureaucratic vultures are hunkering down in the wings with their fat biros gripped, ready to gleefully put a big fat black cross in the box. Which is why when a student came up to Tom two days before the trip and asked him the following question the pens must have been quivering;

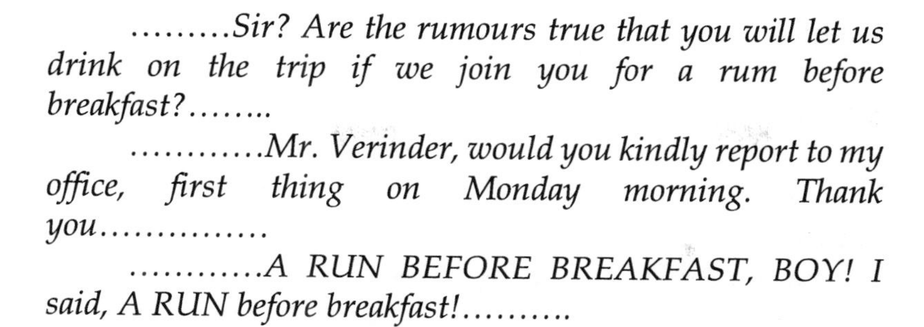

.........Sir? Are the rumours true that you will let us drink on the trip if we join you for a rum before breakfast?........

...........Mr. Verinder, would you kindly report to my office, first thing on Monday morning. Thank you..............

...........A RUN BEFORE BREAKFAST, BOY! I said, A RUN before breakfast!..........

It occurred to me, thinking about this, that the reason the lad thought Tom may actually have set this challenge is because Tom has reached that difficult to attain status of teacher legendary-ness. This status can only be achieved through time – at least two decades – and through a subtle mix of utter down-to-earth approachable ordinariness and off the scale, crazy madness. This crazy madness does not necessarily need to be evidenced but can be rumoured or hinted at, but the potential must absolutely be believed in. This boy actually thought it was possible, and reasonable, that Tom would – pirate like – actually be partaking of a snifter of the strong stuff as an extra-curricular challenge before his buttered croissants. Absolutely brilliant.

Actually, thinking on this further, going for a run before breakfast was probably no less obscure a challenge to the lad than talking of the high seas with Mr. V over a glass of Captain Morgan.

Chapter 66.

Rhu-de-barb

Every year it happens. Sometimes it lasts a few days, sometimes longer. Tom's Paris malaise. It's understandable I suppose. Here is a choice; Paris – dripping with romantic and cultural ambiance and significance; or Wakefield. Mmmm, let me think.
This time it's particularly bad though. Hemingway in hand, Tom spends hours staring wistfully out of the window. Comparisons are cruel; no, Wakefield Westgate is not the Gare-du-Nord. The Bull ring does not remind me of Montmartre. Belle View is not comparable to the Stade de France. Paris based English speaking schools have been perused. A Paris break in May has been booked. He is hurting.

It's time to act. Tom clearly needs help. And I know what I need to do.

Rhubarb to the rescue.

Yes, Paris, I said, Rhubarb. Wakefield Gold. We are talking one corner of the rhubarb triangle, right here. I need to plan carefully. Bring Tom back to his senses; to his true love of West Yorkshire step by step. Frogs legs will be dead to him by the time I have finished.

First step; to Wakefield's rhubarb festival. Amazing stalls selling everything you ever wanted made with rhubarb and plenty you didn't. A bottle of rhubarb gin glowing in his hand and a packet of

Wakefield's seasonal sweet ruby strands and things are already looking up.

Next step; to the brilliant retrospective of Martin Parr's photographs at the Hepworth Gallery. Yes, Paris, Wakefield has an art gallery; a whole room of vivid reds, blues and whites documenting Wakefield's history as the epicentre of forced rhubarb production. Who knew? No frames, (or God forbid, glass fronts, Mona) just pinned to the wall as if they are about to be taken down any minute, making it seem even more immediate. Parr documents brilliantly those who take themselves too seriously, showing them as ugly, garish and laughable – middle class England in the 80's, public school aspiring, middle England, Southern detached house pretentiousness – while documenting those who don't give themselves a second thought, seriously and allegorically – working class Calderdale, Northern holiday resorts in the baking sun, the demise of the industrial North. Wakefield gets the serious treatment. Tom loved it. Stage two complete.

Next, to the pub; a great new bar opened quietly in the centre of Wakefield. No coffee and no Carlsberg in sight. Yes, the ubiquitous beard behind the bar but he can be forgiven because he knows his beer. He is running the kind of pub a woman who has a book to read and a thirst to quench can have a quiet drink in, without feeling exposed. And why not, Paris? This is culture too. Plus, he has a guest beer; Rhubarbarella. 7.4%. Not a session ale. Tom has a half pint taster and his cheeks turn the colour of rhubarb. Stage three complete.

And finally to stage four; the week's food, bought at the brilliant farmer's market, obviously and aptly named 'The Rhubarb Triangle' – what else. A proper Yorkshire tea ensues; topped perfectly with a fine rhubarb crumble and custard. Yesterday's confit de canard is a distant memory.

And as a final epitaph to forgotten France; I notice something that makes me chuckle. A fridge face-off; a jar of Foie Gras de Canard Entier; unopened. Next to it is a half scooped jar of Pork Pie and Rhubarb Chutney. No contest. I rest my case. Tom is returned to me.

For another year at least.

Chapter 67.

Some Luck

I walked to the hospital today. It was a lovely clear blue late Winter (early Spring?) morning. I walked with a new juicy fat book in hand; Jane Smiley's *Some Luck* to distract me – I hadn't thought of the irony of that until now. I moved considerably faster than the poor commuters crawling solo in their cars. A major accident had brought Wakefield to a standstill. I bet more than one or two of them took a glance at me as I sauntered past their wound up windows. 'Look at that bloody woman.' I bet they thought, 'strolling without a care in the world with her book. Where is she going? Not to work. Off to read her book and drink tea in a cafe somewhere, I bet. Lazy cow. Maybe have her hair done in the afternoon, maybe her nails.' WRONG! I am actually off to the slightly less enjoyable experience of having £6,000 worth of cutting edge chemo drugs drip, drip, dripped into my hand from a garish green plastic pouch. I think that you poor commuters may just edge it on me today.

On the plus side, it went much better this time. The precarious concoction of chemo, ant-histamines and steroids was achieved. This prevented me from having a lovely allergic reaction again. Having one unexpected is bad enough, waiting for one to happen can put you a bit on edge to say the least.

Released by mid-day, I didn't have my nails done or my hair (obviously) but I did read my book in a lovely cafe and drink tea all afternoon. So on reflection, screw you commuters. I win.

Chapter 68.

Costume Drama

Now that I am having to face into my single breasted future I have extended my wardrobe. I am now the proud owner of 2 x bras, 2 x sport bras and 2 x swimming costumes. My new swimming purchases double my previous collection. My trusty, tired speedo is now redundant. I realised, to my horror, that I have had this costume for over 20 years. Considering how infrequently I go swimming, mind, this is not as ridiculous as it sounds. My new swimming costumes are a whole new world. I suspect that they have not been designed with swimming in mind. According to my lovely brochure, in my new costume I will be able to *amp up my poolside look and channel my inner 1950's starlet.* No less. The amount of tassels, trimming and inner corseting going on, I doubt I'll be able to do a nifty 50 lengths in it anyway. Reclining, looking demure and ensuring my nail polish matches may be the sum total of my capabilities which is fine with me anyway. And of course the main feature is its nifty little pocket for my prosthetic to snuggle securely in. 'Cossy' and 'prossy' upon first try-on look mighty fine to me.

A weekend away at a Spa Hotel in Newcastle did, however, give them a sterner test beyond the aesthetic. First test; a light swim. No issues. No escapee right boob bobbing away and alarming any fellow swimmers. To the Jacuzzi next. If things didn't work out here there could be an injury. A flying prosthetic powered by turbo ejected jet streams could probably do some real damage. Again, my session passed without incident. And so finally to the ultimate test; the sauna. What are prosthetic boobs made of? I presume its silicon. Can they melt in high temperatures? Who knows? I didn't think the lovely Geordie chap I got chatting to in there quite deserved the vision of my right breast gradually turning into something from Terminator. Anyway, it didn't happen. 'Prossy' and 'cossy' both passed with flying colours. I am mighty pleased as I very much like saunas.

Saunas are, however, peculiar places. I have noticed that, the obvious intimacy of sitting, sweating, half naked with people you don't know seems to draw out conversation. The best, and most enlightening chat I ever had was in my old gym sauna with a chap in his late 50's who opened the conversation with the line,

"Right, love, what do you want to talk about? Weddings or Rugby League?"

I have no doubt that if I had plumped for the former he would have had plenty to say on the subject but in the event we spent an enjoyable half hour bemoaning the plight of Wakefield Wildcats position at the bottom of the Super League table.

My favourite pass time in saunas is to guess how many people will enter the sauna during my stay and proclaim surprisedly, "Oohh, my goodness! It is hot in here!" My best ever is 8 out of 10.

Probably the funniest moment I have had in a sauna was with my two sisters a few years back. We had booked ourselves into the very expensive and very refined Ragdale Hall, a lovely hotel and spa retreat. The first time myself and my twin sister went, as we turned the corner up the drive we looked at each other in horror as we realised, this was the kind of place where guests walked dreamily hand in hand around the grounds in white slippers and bath robes and fell asleep outside in posh deck chairs. Yes. it was. We had to chuckle two days later when we found ourselves sitting outside in white slippers and bath robes dropping into a deep post massage sleep without a care in the world. It also had a fantastic range of saunas and steam rooms. This particular sauna was dark and lit only by two blue neon strip lights, the other sauna goers were only just visible beyond the blue mist. However, as my sister sat down the water and air below her formed into a perfect mock-fart formation. The noise, as it rip-echoed round the hard walls of the sauna, was phenomenal. And then silence. Nothing. COME ON!!! It was hilarious! We started to chuckle and then laugh uncontrollably. Our fellow, colonically irrigated guests, didn't seem to find a mighty female fart, no matter how falsely manufactured, remotely funny and remained tight lipped and so we had to make our escape. We didn't return to the neon sauna again.

Chapter 69.

Not a Running Joke

My amazing sister is running a half marathon next month. Don't be tricked by the 'half' bit of this endeavour. 13 and a bit miles is a very, very long way to run. She is taking part in the first ever Manchester half marathon and raising money for Royal Manchester Children's Hospital. The race is described on the official website as, *a super-fast, flat course with great entertainment, outstanding crowd support and a glorious finish at Lancashire Cricket Club.* They make is sound like a nice day trip out round the sites of Manchester. Oh, ok, not a grueling 20k+ slog at all, then?

I have run my fair share of 5ks, 10ks, and a few half marathons but only the one marathon. It was a long time ago and to be honest it nearly finished me.

The whole experience started to go horribly wrong the night before. I had travelled down to London to stay with a friend so I would be ready for the 10 o'clock start the next day. I was looking forward to a quiet meal with her and her boyfriend and a nice early bedtime to be prepped for the next day. This is not what I got. Unfortunately for my friend, and as it turned out, for me, she had temporarily split from her boyfriend and moved in with five girlfriends. This was now where I was going to stay too. I am not judging one bit but there was some anger in this house, mainly directed at men. As it approached midnight I realised that my pre-run meal was not going to be forthcoming and as fags and champagne (and bile towards the male species) were the only things on offer I was best to abstain from consuming anything. I dared to suggest at half past one that it might be my bedtime. BED TIME?! What the fuck was that? No-one was going to bed while there was still wine to drink, dope to smoke (and men out there to hate). I stayed quiet. Finally, as it approached 2.30 am, I was getting desperate and demanded that I at least needed to lie down somewhere as I had the small matter of running a very long way tomorrow. This went down a bit better and my friend put me up on a mattress in the front room with a throw from the sofa. As I drifted into a vague sleep I pondered whether Paula Radcliffe's pre-run regime involved Marlboro's, marijuana and a mattress.

In the morning I was rescued by my friend's 'estranged' boyfriend and driven into London to my start line. Refreshed I was not. I would have felt better if I had run all the way from Wakefield to London overnight. However, the atmosphere was unbelievable and was the shot of adrenalin I needed. I ran the first 10 miles at a pace that would have seen me finish in under two and half hours. BIG, big mistake. I had done the classic. Shot off like a pro, fueled by the steel bands and well-wishers. I was on fire. At mile 11 I was not on fire. I felt like utter shit. I had 15 and a bit miles to go for Christ sake and all I wanted to do was lie down somewhere really quiet. I needed to get a grip. A friend had told me one way to focus the mind, once the pain kicked in, was to find a nice tight male butt and run behind it. I looked around. 3 rhinos, Mickey Mouse and a seven-foot clown were the best I could do.

At 13 miles the real trauma started. I had trained pretty well in terms of my legs and arms but had totally underestimated the impact of exercising for over 2 hours on my gut. And now my gut was not at all happy. I don't know whether I had taken on too much sports drink or it was the nerves but my insides were turning volcanic. It was around about 16 miles that I had to accept that running and clenching was not going to suffice. I took the first of many pit stops in a pub. What I had to do was not for the portaloos scattered randomly along the way and definitely not for the road side. The pubs I visited on that day were all packed with lovely, sane, happy people, drinking beer, watching football and laughing with friends and family. I hated them all.

Around about the 18th mile I decided I was going to give up. My stomach was a disaster and I couldn't feel my legs below mid-thigh. What supporters don't realise about the London Marathon is that you don't need a bloody steel band and rousing cheering at mile 1 when you are feeling fantastic, you need them at mile 18 when you know you are definitely going to die. However, at mile 18 you're running under deserted underpasses and along ugly empty streets. Not a soul is cheering you on through the wall. It is utterly depressing.

I didn't stop, though, because I didn't have the faintest idea where I was. Plus, once you hit mile 20 you are slightly delirious, anyway. The numbness had crept to waist height which gave me the not unpleasant feeling that I was floating. But there is no denying that when you hit the pink tarmac of the final mile straight you do feel emotional. As you cross the line, just for an infinitesimal split second, you think that it has all been worth it. Then the proper pain kicks in.

I collapsed on a grassy hillside and folded myself into a foetal position and sobbed quietly to myself. To my disgust next to me was a group of 6 or 7 men, at least in their 60's, doing a sprightly warm down that involved star jumps. Who has ever done star jumps as a warm down, never mind after running 26 fucking miles? When they were all suitably warmed down, one of them sat nimbly next to me, smiled smugly and proceeded to produce from his light weight rucksack the whitest, fluffiest, softest, most desirable pair of clean fresh socks I had ever seen.

"Any runner worth his salt will have brought a spare pair of running socks!" he said.

My sobbing was becoming difficult to control now. Could I bash him over the head with my empty bottle of Evian and do a runner with his socks? As I watched him lasciviously peal his fresh socks onto his grateful feet I had to look away.

My feet were now indiscernible from my socks, which had dried and hardened into a kind of cotton plaster-of-Paris consistency around and in-between my toes. I had blisters on my blisters and my left big toe nail had cut into its neighbor, leaving a dark blood stain in my trainer. Lovely. My feet were not my worst injury. Running for too long creates even more pleasant bodily malfunctions. I had laughed out loud at the beginning of the race when I saw a lanky club runner putting plasters over his nipples. What the hell? It was only a marathon, how bad was it going to get? I also declined the lovely policemen and women handing out globules of Vaseline at the start line. Where were people putting it? Little did I know. My running bra had cut two lovely holes below each boob where it had rubbed. Tit plaster man had had the last laugh on me. I had also bought a new pair of running shorts that I had never worn before. 26 miles of running had evidenced that these shorts had two rough seams running down the inside of each leg which had created two beautiful friction burns down each thigh. I was a total mess. And that was just on the outside.

The final insult to my lovely day out was that I had organised to meet my friend from work who was also running. After two and half hours waiting for her, however, she was no longer my friend. At no point had she ever bothered to tell me that she intended to STROLL the London Marathon rather than run the bloody thing. She finally tripped up, fresh as a daisy, while I had, during the intervening hours, now seized up so badly I had to be levered, like a piece of 4 by 4, into a standing position.

My friend's friend drove us back to Wakefield. A BIG mistake; I am sure if the Queen had lent me her private driver and limo it would have been a painful journey but my friend's friend, drove like she was driving a motorbike. Before changing gear, she revved the car to the point of no return, changed gear and then nearly stalled it; every time. This made the car lurch and rock and me slowly begin to realise that today was never going to end. To make things worse she spent the whole trip on her phone and this was the days before hands-free.

When I finally got home, I cried a bit more. We lived, at that time, in a basement flat. It only had two, very small steps up from the kitchen into the bedroom. It took me over 20 minutes to negotiate these before collapsing into bed and into a painful sleep.

Good luck, sis, you'll be fine. After all it's only a half marathon.

Chapter 70.

No Vein No Gain

I had my sixth and final round of chemotherapy yesterday. Hoorah! Straight forward once we got going with the small matter of finding an open and willing vein in my hand. This small, but essential procedure, took 2 hours and 6 attempts. It appeared that my veins had had enough and had decided to securely shut up shop to all needles and nurses. This is a slight inconvenience given that an intravenous drip is, so far, the only way medical science has come up with to administer my particular strain of chemotherapy. Anyway, the first nurse assigned to me took one look at my vein-less hand and delegated immediately to another colleague; a wise move on her part. The lovely second nurse in situ did not fill me with much more positivity. Two attempts later and she delegated upwards again. Colleague number three didn't even pretend to look enticed by the prospect of prodding aimlessly at my increasingly bruised and bloodied hand and proceeded to add another FAIL x 2 to my medical notes. It was time for the Sister. She had a few tried and tested tricks up her sleeve – namely to run my hand under boiling water and then get me to run across the ward for needle number five. It didn't work. It was getting a bit serious now. My out of bounds right arm was now being considered. I was not a fan of this conversation. Given the important job of your lymph nodes in clearing waste product from round your body and my notable lack of any on my right side, I feared this was the less than ideal plan B. So my Sister took a deep breath, I closed my eyes, clenched my fist and looked away for the sixth time as the needle moved away from the battle ground that was my hand and into my virginal wrist. Success; in and open and good to flow. A pretty picture of my hand in my medical notes would now have FAIL x 5 scrawled all over it.

Two hours later I was free to go, feeling fine except for the fact that I was laden down with the biggest stash of take home drugs I had ever seen;

Dexamethasone 2mg – 8 a day (steroids – trick your brain into thinking nothing is going on – make you feel hot and bloated and irritable – like a teenager, basically).

Ondansetron 8mg – 2 day (ant- sickness – don't feel sick but will take them anyway).

Cetirizine Hydrochloride 1mg – 1 a day (ant- histamines – help against allergic reaction to the chemo and conveniently sort out my hay fever at the same time).

Fluconazole 50mg – 1 a day (helps keeps lovely oral thrush at bay and prevents travel to less than convenient places further down digestive tract – all food tastes like flour).

Nystatin Oral Suspension – 4 spoonful's a day (As above – but tastes hideous).

Filgrastim subcutaneous syringes – 1 jab a day (Injected by me into fat of stomach – helps bone marrow to produce more white blood cells to combat the ones being blasted by chemo – doesn't hurt much but looks brave and brutal).

Pain killers – as required – 2 a day (to combat all side effects of above).

In the few spare minutes left to me when I am not swallowing down copious amounts of prescription drugs I am going out for a long walk to celebrate day one of my post-chemo era. I am feeling very buoyant.

Chapter 71.

The Tiniest Tattoos in the World

I had a CT scan today. Not in order to diagnose anything, just to help my radiologist target her gamma rays at the right parts of me. The actual procedure took approximately eight and a half minutes.

Unfortunately, driving to St James Hospital in Leeds, finding a parking space, finding the Oncology Department, waiting, waiting, waiting and waiting a bit longer, for my appointment took about two hours.

The first time my name was called out it was to have a five-minute chat with a lovely nurse who took me through the procedure; painless and harmless, two very good words to hear in my view. The second time my name was called out, a very bouncy nurse, with a very loud voice called me out right into the middle of the waiting room to announce that she had a quick question about my treatment.

Amusingly, this question was, “Is it the left or the right side you need treatment for?”

Mmmmm, let me think for a minute. This is a tricky question. Understandably I find remembering which boob is fine and which boob is not there anymore, having been removed, a little difficult! WTF??? It turned out that my Oncologist had written in my notes that it was my left side when all the rest of my medical history said the right side. ‘You can understand we need to be absolutely sure about these kind of things!' Yes, bouncy nurse, you REALLY DO need to be sure. I've only got one bloomin' boob left, leave it alone!

Once this small matter was cleared up I waited another hour before I was finally called in for my scan. I had to lie totally still with my right arm (yes, my RIGHT arm) above my head while two nurses measured, marked and taped me up before I was motored slowly through the middle of a huge plastic polo mint.

When this was finished I was then given three tattoos. One on my sternum, one on my right collar bone and one under my right arm. If the definition of a tattoo is a permanent mark on the skin that is created by using needles to put colour under the skin, then I now have three tattoos on my torso. The fact that they are only just perceivable with the naked eye is beside the point. I am now a tattooed lady. As the nurses need to target the radiology in exactly the same place for all fifteen rounds, they need a permanent mark. As I am only going to have radiotherapy for three weeks rather than every day for the rest of my life, I fail to see why an impermanent marker wouldn't do the job but there we go.

I am a big fan of tattoos. Not the unimaginative insipid dolphin on the ankle or the heart torn thorny rose on the bicep. I am a talking the full torso, full limb, full coloured, off the scale, tattoos; when tattoos really transform the body into an art form. For example, there is a guy at my gym who swims length after length of beautiful butterfly strokes. His back and arms are 100%

tattoo-ed. They appear to be a tattoo tribute to Henri Rousseau which I think is brilliant. As he glides in and out of the water it is quite mesmeric to watch as 'Tiger in a Tropical Storm (surprised!)' submerges and emerges at each stroke. It is all I can do to resist going up to him to see whether I can spot David Attenborough peeping out from behind his shoulder blades.

Many women actually opt for tattoos to cover up their mastectomy scars. One lady, I have seen a photo of, has flowers and butterflies tattooed all over her right side. It looks strangely beautiful. I can understand this but I am not remotely tempted. For now, I am content with my three dots. In the future, if I am feeling adventurous, I might have a tattoo artist join them up with three dark pink lines in tribute to the Wakefield Rhubarb Triangle. Now there's a thought.

Chapter 72.

For Whom the Bell Tolls

Guess what you have to do when you have finished your fifteen blasts of radiotherapy? Ring a bloody bell. Can you believe it? It's clearly not enough to have had most of your physical dignity stripped to the point where you now resemble a naked mole rat minus the buck teeth. Now I must stand lepra-esque in my back to front gown and dutifully chime the bell of cancer victory. Well, I'm not going to do it. I am a major fan of the NHS but whoever came up with this idea needs a short sharp smack. Bell ringing reminds me of three things; weddings, funerals and the end of playtime. Bell ringing should never have anything to do with modern cancer treatment; ever. At least it explains why, every now and again in the waiting, waiting and more waiting room I heard the toll of a bell and everyone spontaneously burst into a round of clapping and cheering. I hadn't got a clue what they were clapping for. I just presumed a fund raising target had been hit or something.

There was a girl in my class at school who did bell ringing as a hobby at the weekend. As narrow minded, cruel early-teenagers, my friends and I took the merciless piss out of her. I can't remember her name but I do remember she was very straight and played the bassoon. Bell ringing and bassoon playing in a state school is more than enough ammunition to bag your place as the class victim of female bullying, I am afraid. Obviously, to our nasty teenage narrow minds this quiet, studious, uninterested in boys, girl was obviously a lesbian and therefore when we discovered, to our joy, that the art of bell ringing is called Campanology we were beside ourselves. I am not proud.

Years later I met her when I was a tired and stressed buyer at lowly Asda. She swanned in as a supplier for an internationally-renowned wine merchant, to see one of my colleagues. Five foot eleven, long legged, blonde and gloriously stunning she just about condescended to remember me. We had an awkward five-minute conversation about French vintages which I knew very little about and she clearly knew a great deal about and then she was gone in a flounce of expensive perfume and designer trouser. I didn't dare ask her whether she still liked to dabble in a spot of Campanology of the weekend. Oh well.

I am still not going to ring that fucking bell.

Chapter 73.

Please Proceed to Gate 22

I have just booked flights to Tenerife for an extended break for some much needed R&R in the warm sun of the Canary Islands. I cannot wait.

This time when I am called to Gate 22 (or whichever gate number it happens to be – I don't really care) I won't be in Pinderfields Hospital atrium, masquerading as an airport, I will be in the real thing. And this time I will be able to have a cheeky beer on the way through, and I will pick up a light holiday read. Because this time, on the other side of the gate there will be no cancer treatment drugs waiting for me but rather a short haul aeroplane warming up nicely on the tarmac to take me away from it all. I deserve it and so do my family. It is finally finished but I am not.

The End